BLOODY SUNDAY

BLOODY SUNDAY

How Michael Collins's Agents
Assassinated Britain's Secret Service
in Dublin on November 21, 1920

James Gleeson

Introduction by Dermot McEvoy

THE LYONS PRESS
GUILFORD, CONNECTICUT
AN IMPRINT OF THE GLOBE PEQUOT PRESS

Dedicated to

Eve

Timothy

Theresa Ann

Mary B.

Patrick

Katherine

CONTENTS

Foreword by W. R. Rodgers   ix

Acknowledgments   xiv

Introduction by Dermot McEvoy   xvii

 1 The Rebel City   1

 2 The Forces of the Crown   5

 3 After the Surrender   30

 4 Guerilla Warfare   39

 5 The Auxiliary's Story   56

 6 Tudor's Toughs   79

 7 The Murder Gangs   101

 8 The Passing of "The Particular Ones"   128

 9 Massacre by the Black and Tans   143

10 Murder Most Foul   151

11 The Following Day   170

12 The Day the Liffey Ran Black with Hats   183

13 The Simple Answer   198

Sources   210

ILLUSTRATIONS

Map of Morehampton Road area, Dublin, for attack   xii
on house marked "X" in which were British Secret
Service men. Prepared before operations of Sunday
morning, November 21, 1920, by donor Mr. J. E. Lynch.

Facing page

Daylight landing of rifles for the Irish Volunteers   52
Erskine Childers

Michael Collins   53
Tom Barry

A typical group of the IRA   84

Men who helped to annihilate the British Intelligence   85

The men the IRA were fighting   148

The Tipperary Football Team who played at Croke Park   149

Auxiliaries searching a Post Office van   180
The funeral of two British Intelligence Officers

Ben and Kathleen Doyle   181
Paddy Moran and Thomas Whelan

FOREWORD

W. R. RODGERS

"At last I succeeded in overtaking the whale, I quickly launched a well-sharpened and solid harpoon (after having first made fast and checked the rope); the harpoon darted, penetrated far into the flesh, making an enormous wound. I realized then that I was the whale, I had changed into it again, there was a new opportunity to suffer, and I am not one to get used to suffering."

My Properties by Henri Michaux. Trans. by R. Ellmann

Those of us who grew up in Ireland during the Troubles are not likely to forget the experience. The time, the place, the antagonists were alive and bleeding; they had not yet hardened in the rigor mortis of history. How to convey the ambience of that violence—the gunshot in the dark, feet running, the frightened silence—is the whale of a problem that we hunt and are haunted by. Occasionally we try to put it down in a book in the hope that by recounting it to others we may recover it for ourselves. James Gleeson, the author of this book, is a case in point, and his family background so well reflects the tensions of the time that I make no apology for telling it here. Being a diffident man, Gleeson may not like this, but his father's son will not mind.

James Gleeson was reared in County Waterford, in the village of Tallow where his father was sergeant in charge of the Royal Irish Constabulary barracks. James remembers hearing Cathal Brugha speak: and recalls how it was part of his father's duty to go to the town pump and read out the news of important political happenings; in this way he learned about the defeat of the in-

surgents in the Easter Week Rising of 1916. There was no trouble
in Tallow while Gleeson's father was in charge, for he was liked
and respected by everyone. Yet the underlying tensions were
strong. A regular visitor to Tallow was the butter-buyer, and James,
as a boy, used to help him, for half-a-crown a day, to test the
water-content of the farmers' butter. Long afterwards he learned
that the butter-buyer was the I R A liaison-officer for the area.
It was the butter-buyer's nephew, Constable Creedon, who figured
notably in a local incident. Captured one night by I R A raiders
he was forced at the gunpoint to precede them to the door of
Tallow Barracks and ask admission. "Don't open!" shouted Constable Creedon to the police within. "It's the I R A!" "Don't
shoot him!" ordered an I R A voice behind him, and, with a
warning shot through the door, the raiders departed.

Like other boys, Gleeson used to play hurley in the street. He
possessed a proud hurley-stick, cut from an ash tree with the grain
running with the bend. One day a Black-and-Tan borrowed the
stick to try his skill but accidentally struck it against the kerb,
breaking the boss of the stick. The boy was heart-broken, so the
Black-and-Tan after vainly trying to console him with money,
took the broken stick to the carpenter at the local mill. But the
carpenter refused to mend it for the carpenter happened to be
the local commandant of the I R A. Politics touched rawly on life
at many points, even on a child's life. At holiday-times the boy
would go to visit his Tipperary uncles who were confirmed Republicans and who recalled for him how *their* uncle, a locksmith
in Manchester, had sawed the handcuffs off Captain Deasey who
had escaped from the prison-van and for whom the Manchester
Martyrs had died. The tensions of the times were not only public
but private ones.

In 1919 Gleeson's father, promoted to the head-constable, was
transferred to Lanesborough, County Longford: on the night he
left Tallow the first I R A attack on Tallow Barracks took place.
Head-Constable Gleeson was a champion revolver-and-rifle shot of
the Royal Irish Constabulary, but in Tallow he would never carry
revolver or rifle with him. He was a firm disciplinarian who strongly
disapproved of the excesses of the Black-and-Tans and Auxiliaries
with whom he was obliged to work. Once, when two lorry-loads

of Auxiliaries came to Lanesborough Barracks he ordered them to leave his district. After some argument they left, but, forty yards away, they stopped and, with a final angry volley, shot the chimneys off the barracks. Another day, patrolling with twelve constables and two Black-and-Tans, Head-Constable Gleeson was ambushed and one of the Black-and-Tans killed. That night, the Auxiliaries arrived in Lanesborough to take reprisals. Several prominent citizens, including the local doctor, were put against a wall to be shot but the head-constable stood between them and their executioners and managed to save their lives. Immediately afterwards he resigned from the Royal Irish Constabulary. The human dilemma had become insufferable.

The author of the book, like his father, is a temperate man though he told me one day that he had knocked a man down. "I was surprised at myself," he said, "but when I was introduced to him he asked me casually if I were one of the 'Gleeson helpers', and those, as you know, are fighting words in Tipperary." "I don't know," I said. "Tell me." He told me. The story goes that when Oliver Cromwell was going through Ireland with his plundering army he came to a long hill in North Tipperary called Craughshana Hill. His horses tried vainly to drag the heavy seige-artillery up the hill. So Cromwell at length commandeered other horses from the nearest Irish farm which happened to belong to the Gleesons. The Irish horses pulled the guns over the top. Ever since that day, if you want to annoy a Gleeson you have only to inquire if he is one of "the Gleeson helpers". In Ireland the myth always takes over from the man, the myth in which victor and victim continue to change places and exchange sufferings. We are not the ones to get used to suffering, and this book *Bloody Sunday* is a necessary attempt to disentangle some part of the myth from the terrible reality.

W. R. R.

Leeson St Bridge

Burlington Rd

Wilton Rd

More

Canal

Leeson Church

Upper Mount

Rd to City

Road

opperations Sunday morning at

Nov 21st 1920

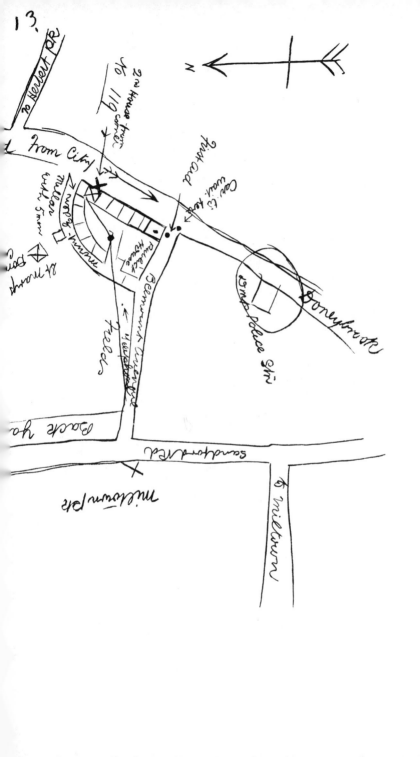

13.

ACKNOWLEDGEMENTS

Much that is contained in *Bloody Sunday* is the result of conversations held over the past forty years, much that I saw for myself, and much that I have read.

The British Government has been of little help. There is a rule—proved of course by the exception—that fifty years must pass before certain papers become available to the public.

A great deal has been written by Irishmen on "the troubles", very little by ex-members of the British forces in Ireland during that period. That is understandable. The fight for Irish independence was a major event to the people of Ireland but merely an incident in the history of British Imperialism. The overwhelming mass of the British people were, in fact, hardly interested at all in what was happening in Ireland. The Anglo-Irish were deeply interested; so were the bigoted planter class of Northern Ireland, as were the British ruling classes and the "huntin', fishin' and shootin' " fraternities. These, generically known in Ireland as "The Ascendancy", were horrified at the possibility of the Irish people winning long denied independence.

Field Marshal Sir Henry Wilson: His Life and Diaries by General C. E. Callwell, *Annals of an Active Life* by General Macready and *Winter's Tale* by Sir Ormonde Winter give the embittered Ascendancy side of the picture. *Britain between the Wars* by Charles Loch Mowat gives an excellent summing-up of the struggle—the result of extensive research carried out in an expert way into the enormous mass of material which has been published on the subject.

The Black and Tans by Richard Bennett is a well written account of that infamous body but it leans towards the official communiqué and he finds it hard to stomach some of the accounts of British atrocities—which Englishman does not? Rex Taylor in *Michael Collins* has written an excellent and scholarly account of Collins and his times and one which will always be an important one in the annals of Irish history.

Of the Irish writers, David Hogan in *Four Glorious Years* recaptures vividly and authentically the spirit and atmosphere of those years, and Ernie O'Malley's *On Another Man's Wounds* is a superbly written account of his own experiences as an I R A leader. Charlie Dalton's book *With the Dublin Brigade* is a stirring account of I R A activity in the capital and Robert Brennan's *Allegiance* is another outstanding account of the events of that period. One of the most valuable contributions to the history of those times is the series of books published by *The Kerryman*, the accounts in this series being written by the participants themselves soon after the end of hostilities.

Max Caulfield is preparing a history of the Irish Rebellion of 1916 which promises to be one of the most valuable works on that subject. He was very helpful. General Pieras Beaslai, Michael Noyk, Cathal O'Shannon, and Liam O'Breen were gracious enough to allow me to listen in on their reminiscences. Jack Shouldice spared no effort to ensure that I was provided with authentic material about events in Dublin, and Ben Doyle went to enormous trouble to check and confirm the facts of his own experiences which appear in this book. Other Irish people who helped were Bridie McGlone, Jack Scally, Tom and Terry Sheehy, Seamus Kavanagh, Paddy Hanley,

Paul Dolin, James Kenny, Bill Kavanagh, Rory O'Connor. They helped in various ways in Dublin and London, assisting me in tracing genuine participants, confirming or demolishing stories of the period, or in the dull business of preparing the manuscript. The late Mick Power, who fought in the Waterford I R A, spared no effort to help in Dublin; neither did Pat Radford, an Englishman, in London. Bill Munro, the ex-Auxiliary Highlander, allowed me to use his story as he wrote it, knowing that it would stick out like the proverbial sore thumb. James O'Beirne spent what I thought was a fascinating day telling me about the life and trials of an I R A man between 1919 and 1921.

I have used the verbatim accounts of newspapers of the time—*The Times*, the *Daily Telegraph*, the *Daily News*, the *Manchester Guardian*, the *Morning Post* and the *Spectator*— and to these papers I wish to give grateful acknowledgement.

I should like to thank the staffs of the National Museum of Ireland and the National Library of Ireland who treated my every request with courtesy and affability, as did the ladies of the B B C picture library and Gael-linn in Dublin.

Finally, there is a saying in Ireland, usually in Gaelic, which goes: "An old woman told me that an old woman told her that she had seen an old woman who had heard an old woman say that she had seen Patrick with his mouth open." I am grateful to all the old women.

INTRODUCTION

"All I want to lead is sixty determined trustworthy men, and I'll beat the British."

—Michael Collins

There have been many momentous events in the annals of Irish history, but the one that is most responsible for the existence of the Irish Republic today remains cloaked in controversy, mystery, denial, and even shame.

The date was November 21, 1920, and it became known as "Bloody Sunday." (Incidentally, there have been three "Bloody Sundays" in Irish history: one in 1913, when the Dublin Metropolitan Police charged a meeting of Jim Larkin's striking Transport Workers' Union in O'Connell Street; one in 1920, which is the subject of this book; and one in 1971, the most famous, when British troops opened fire on the defenseless citizens of Derry.) On Bloody Sunday 1920, agents of the legendary revolutionary Michael Collins entered buildings in what today is Ireland's most exclusive postal code, Dublin 4, and assassinated the British Secret Service. Fourteen British agents—known as the "Cairo Gang"—fell in front of Collins's men. Later that day in retaliation, the Black and Tans opened fire on a football crowd at Croke Park, killing fourteen citizens, including a Tipperary player.

The effect was immediate. Newspapers in both Britain and Ireland howled about the atrocities, and British politicians denounced the "terrorists." But in one morning Collins's men had blinded British Intelligence in Ireland and sent a resounding message to Prime Minister David Lloyd George. (Weeks later, Lloyd George would tell the truth about the Cairo Gang: "They got what they deserved. Beaten by counter-jumpers.") It would take eight months, but in July 1921 a truce was declared and the two enemies, Collins and Lloyd George—both supreme pragmatists—sat across a table at Number 10 Downing Street and hammered out a treaty, which was signed on December 6, 1921. After seven hundred years, the British had departed forever from twenty-six of Ireland's thirty-two counties.

In *Bloody Sunday*, author James Gleeson gives a gripping account of that mild November day. Amazingly, this book has been out of print for forty-two years. Initially published in London by Peter Davies Ltd. in 1962, *Bloody Sunday* was apparently allowed to vanish in the U.K. and Ireland and, as far as can be determined, was never even published in the United States. This is extraordinary because it is a seminal historic work mentioned in the bibliography of every important book on Michael Collins and the War of Independence. This is the only book that deals exclusively with the events of that Sunday, what precipitated the action, and what political repercussions resulted. So why has it been out of print so long? The simple reason might be that modern Ireland—the land of the Celtic Tiger—is loathe to acknowledge how it was conceived in terrorism, and Great Britain is still reluctant to be reminded of how it propagated its own brand of terrorism in the form of the Black and Tans. Before this Lyons Press edition, scholars could only find *Bloody Sunday* in such places as the National Library in Dublin, the main branch of the New York Public Library, or, if they were lucky, on the Internet.

Gleeson lays the framework leading up to the events of Bloody Sunday. For the uninitiated, he tells how the British came to Ireland and he describes the long litany of rebellions that failed to remove them. He gives an extensive history of the Easter Rebellion of 1916 and shows how out of that debacle Michael Collins invented the IRA and built up an intelligence network that was second to none. According to Gleeson, Collins was tipped off by a contact he had in Scotland Yard that intelligence agents were assembling in Dublin for the express purpose of destroying Collins and his intelligence network. It was decided that all the British agents, who lived outside the safe confines of Dublin Castle, would be assassinated at exactly 9 AM on November 21. Collins's personal bodyguard and assassination squad, nicknamed the Twelve Apostles, did the dirty work. However, the operation was on such a large scale that other members of the Dublin Brigade were brought in—probably near the sixty "trustworthy men" that Collins envisioned as a remedy to Ireland's ills.

The operation started out precariously, as two of Collins's closest associates with intimate knowledge of the plan, Dick McKee and Peadar Clancy, were captured at a safe-house the Saturday night before, taken to Dublin Castle, and tortured to death without revealing a thing. Ben Doyle, who was also a guest of the Crown at Dublin Castle that night, reports exactly what happened in a chapter entitled "Murder Most Foul."

In graphic detail Gleeson chronicles what happened at each address on the 21st. For those who saw Neil Jordan's film *Michael Collins*, they will recognize Rosie, the wastepaper pilfering maid at 28 Upper Pembroke Street, who turned out to be one of Collins's most important agents on that dreadful day. And although Gleeson does not mention Collins's assassins by name, there are some very prominent personalities. There was seventeen-year-old Charlie Dalton, who was supposed to collect intelligence papers, but who dashed out of the house with the shooters in the horror of the moment. Dalton would later write a gripping chronicle of Dublin in the time of Collins in his excellent memoir *With the Dublin Brigade*. Also prominent that morning was the genial and colorful Vinnie Byrne, who before his death in 1992 would offer extraordinary firsthand accounts of how Collins used his squad and how the events of Bloody Sunday unfolded. Also among the assassins that morning was a quiet, dark-haired twenty-three-year-old who would be *Taoiseach* (prime minister) of Ireland when President Kennedy visited in 1963. Seán Lemass, perhaps because of his close association with Eamon DeValera—who was in America when Bloody Sunday occurred—did not like to mention that he had worked for Collins on that day. In John Horgan's biography, *Seán Lemass: The Enigmatic Patriot,* when Lemass is asked why he won't speak about his participation on Bloody Sunday, the *Taoiseach* succinctly replies, "Firing squads don't have reunions."

In the last decade there has been rampant speculation about Michael Collins's romantic relationships with various women, other than his fiancée Kitty Kiernan. In *Hazel: A Life of Lady Lavery 1880-1935,* Sinéad McCoole reveals the intimacy Collins shared with Lady Lavery and brings to light for the first time two of Collins's love poems. And Vincent MacDowell conjectures in *Michael Collins and the Brotherhood* that Collins sired two children by another woman. However, one of the startling personal revelations about Collins in *Bloody Sunday* never revealed before is that he planned to break off his engagement to Kitty Kiernan. When asked what he was doing with a woman's fur coat, Collins replied, "It's a breaking-off present for the girl I was going to marry. I must break it off because I don't want her to marry a corpse . . . ." Apparently, Collins changed his mind, because he was still engaged to Kitty when he was assassinated on August 22, 1922.

Perhaps Bloody Sunday is best put into perspective by the words of Michael Collins as quoted by Gleeson: "By their destruction the very air is made sweeter. That should be the future judgment on this particular event. For myself my conscience is clear. There is no crime in detecting and destroying, in war time, the spy and the informer. They have destroyed without trial. I have paid them back in their own coin."

When Michael Collins paid the British back, Ireland became a nation once again.

Dermot McEvoy
December 8, 2003

THE REBEL CITY

E u r o p e ' s most talkative capital was quiet that morning. The reassuring tolling of church bells and the cries of wheeling seagulls, on their perpetual patrol over the rebel city, were the only sounds that disturbed the silence of what was also, in 1920, Europe's most unruly capital.

Some hours before the bells had begun their call to prayer—in the dead silence of the night—men had quietly left their beds, dressed by candlelight and stolen from their homes. They were young men, most of them not yet thirty, many of them under twenty. They dressed alike in belted trench-coats and trilby hats. The trench-coat, a belted rain coat with capacious pockets, was a useful garment for men such as these: its many loose folds hid the bulge—the bulge that was at once the key to a nation's freedom and the instrument of a nation's will.

These men, the soldiers of a guerilla army, now moved quietly through the dark, silent and deserted streets of their familiar Dublin. They walked carefully and in the shadows because it was risky to be abroad at that hour in a city which was beleaguered by a powerful army that sat within its gates—an alien army, an angry army. They were moving into action. Action that climaxed with horrifying finality month after month of careful planning; that scandalized Britain, astonished the world and assured the final victory of Ireland's age-old fight against its ancient enemy.

From all over the city and its suburbs on that mild November morning the men converged. As they met and merged, silent groups materialized. Few words were spoken because the need for speech did not exist then; each man knew the part he was about to play in this macabre drama. The execution squads of the Secret Army met within a well-defined area of the silent city, and now waited nonchalantly—they were that kind of men— for the friendly nod that would send them moving into action.

Fringing this well-defined area were other similarly dressed and pocket-bulging men—the covering force. Theirs was the lesser task and few of them knew what was afoot—they were there in case they should be needed. This was a vital operation and nothing that could be catered for was left to chance. They formed a silent and unobtrusive circle, a patient circle of soldiers no less determined than their colleagues of the execution squads who were now moving off towards the houses where, inside a few terrifying action-packed minutes, a hated force would be shattered and destroyed, a century-old force that had badgered, bedevilled and nullified every previous revolutionary movement of the people of Ireland—the Secret Service of Britain.

At a few minutes to nine o'clock on the morning of Sunday, 21 November, 1920, the execution squads reached their objectives. They stood then before the doors of a number of hotels, boarding-houses, and apartment rooms. Their pockets were not bulging, because the revolvers and automatic pistols that had made the bulges were now firmly gripped in steady hands.

A number of demanding, urgent rat-tats on knockers, and unsuspecting residents opened doors to find groups of quiet men with guns, and the unsuspecting residents became alarmed and nervous ones as the men pushed brusquely past. Sometimes the leader of the group asked a quiet question, sometimes the men seemed to know the house and even the rooms where their targets lay. Quickly, smoothly, efficiently they moved, doors were burst open and the dull bangs of revolvers or the sharp bark of automatic pistols woke the household and the city. Then hurried footsteps retreated, and doors slammed, and only dead and dying Secret Agents remained to prove the reality of the nightmarish visits.

In eight houses on that bloody morning the pattern was repeated with awful monotony—fourteen agents died, five were wounded, and one man in a trench-coat, his trilby hat abandoned, lay by a garden wall with a bullet-shattered leg— a policeman put his revolver against the wounded man's head and began to count up to ten. . . .

That same afternoon in that same unhappy capital 7,000 people gathered to watch a Gaelic football match. A quarter of an hour after the match started the cheers or scoffs of the spectators were drowned by volley after volley of rifle and machine-gun fire. Bullets thudded indiscriminately into the panic-stricken crowd. One of the football players dropped fatally wounded and men, women, and children died or were mutilated in the mayhem.

> "RED SUNDAY IN DUBLIN,
> "RIOT OF DEATH",

were the headlines in the London *Times* on Monday morning.

> "DUBLIN'S RED SUNDAY—
> 14 OFFICERS MURDERED—
> AN ORGANISED BUTCHERY",

the *Morning Post* wrote.

The *Daily News* of 22 November, 1920, told the story in the following words:

"THE TIDAL WAVE OF TERRORISM
Dublin's Day of Massacre
12 Defenceless British Officers Killed in Cold Blood
Total Death Roll 24
Terrible scenes follow panic and stampede at a Football Match

"The greatest outbreak of terrorism yet recorded in Ireland occurred in Dublin yesterday. Simultaneously, in eight separate parts of the city, armed men entered houses where British Officers were residing. In almost all cases the Officers were in bed, and 12 were mercilessly murdered without a chance of defending themselves. It is described as the worst massacre of British Officers since the Indian mutiny. Five other officers and one civilian were wounded. Two police cadets were killed.

"Yesterday afternoon at a football match, shots were fired, a panic ensued and ten persons are reported killed and 60 wounded. Last night it was announced that, from today, a 10 p.m. curfew will come into operation.

"Mr Hugh Martin, Special Correspondent of the *Daily News* who has just returned from Ireland after three months' active investigation of events, points out that yesterday's massacre is the inevitable outcome of a Government's policy of winking at reprisals, and declares that even this terrible harvest will not surprise those who have watched recent developments closely. Dublin, in Mr Martin's opinion, has been for some time past the hiding place of many desperate revolutionaries driven there by military and police 'pressure' in the provinces."

2

THE FORCES OF THE CROWN

I N T H E dim past Britain invaded Ireland and by force of arms occupied it. During 700 years of armed occupation the British did little to earn either the admiration or the respect of the people. Those years were years of sporadic rebellions against the invaders. It was a profitable invasion for the British: Ireland is a fertile land and the overlords enjoyed the fruits of the native labour. The invaders took the rebellions for granted —the peasants were ill-armed, badly organized fellows who could be easily dispersed by a few companies of troops. One time, of course, they had put some kind of organized troops on the field, but Cromwell taught them a salutary lesson with fire and sword to which later invaders added an ingenious, dreadful contraption called a "pitch cap".

The Irish were difficult to understand. After all, the Scots were defeated and, apart from a few irresponsibles who stole the Stone of Scone one Christmas when the English were not looking and gave it back immediately, accepted the British yoke without much ado. The Welsh, apart from swearing at the English in an outlandish tongue, settled down comfortably and, having accepted a Prince, accepted everything else the British liked to give them.

But the Irish!

It proved necessary to keep troops garrisoned at strategic points all over the country, troops who knew and learned little about the inhabitants. The gentry, well armed and well fed, could look after themselves and they entertained themselves in various ways[1]. Lord Doneraile, for instance, used to take an attractive young woman from her family, strip her, smear her with aniseed and turn her into the woods. Later he would release a pack of hounds to pick up the scent of the aniseed and trail the girl. When they found her they would encircle her, baying. The hounds were followed on foot by the noble Lord's guests and the first man to reach the hounds won the young woman—aniseed and all.

These landlords made a good income, which was spent in riotous living in London, from the rents of the farms and houses on their estates, houses which frequently were little more than one-roomed mud huts. The landlords employed land agents to collect the rents and it was the task of these men to push the rent up to the highest possible figure. If the tenant improved his home in any way the agent would increase the rent—so the people obviously did not improve their homes. If they could not pay they were thrown on to the roadside and their hovels burnt. This happened all over Ireland and over one million people were evicted in his way. Still the people kept their friendly nature, as is illustrated by the story of the two evicted men who waited one night behind a hedge to shoot a landlord. The landlord was late and one of the men said to the other, "I hope nothing bad has happened to the poor man."

That too was the era when "praties and point" was the national dish. Meat was very scarce and potatoes—"praties"—by themselves a rather unappetizing dish, so when the family was lucky enough to obtain a small morsel of meat they tied a bit of string around it and dangled it over the table from the ceiling. Each member of the family would rub the bit of meat across their slice of potato and then swing it across to the next member of the family. Eventually times became so bad that even a tiny piece of meat was unobtainable, so the diners had to satisfy themselves with praties alone. They used to "point" them at the place where the little piece of meat used to be.

A type of policeman was raised, called Barony Police, who was paid £4 a year. This wage of 1s 6½d a week did not attract the best kind of man and they were a very villainous lot indeed. In 1815 a very different force was established, called then the Irish Constabulary. These men were, in the rank and file, all Irishmen, and if one ignores the fact that they were the paid agents of the British Government one can well describe them as a magnificent body of men. They were mercenaries—god-fearing and honest mercenaries, courageous, intelligent and loyal to their masters. They were an armed body who lived in barracks in every village and town of Ireland. There has never been much crime in Ireland apart from political ones, so an Irish constable's life was normally a happy one, and as there was little else in Ireland for young men to do for a living, the best and the brightest of the young men joined the police, where they were quickly indoctrinated and trained to act as the eyes and ears of the British Government.

One of their leaders, Sir Thomas Larcom, once wrote[2]: "The police are like a delicate musical instrument responding at once from the remotest part of Ireland to a touch from their Headquarters."

They protected the bums and bailiffs who evicted the families who could not pay their rent, and time and again they quelled rebellious outbursts by the people. One of their famous battles was called the "battle of the cabbage garden at Ballingarry"[3]. It happened in 1848 when a movement called the Young Irelanders decided on open rebellion against the British, who in that era had through indifference and mismanagement allowed a terrible famine to run its course so that millions of Irish died of starvation or left Ireland to find something to eat.

Three thousand of the Young Irelanders, armed mostly with pikes, met near the village of Ballingarry in Co. Tipperary. A constable hurried to where the Inspector of Police, a Mr Blake, was attending a ball ."The rebels are out," gasped the breathless constable, and Mr Blake went at once to the barracks. He sent messengers to other barracks at the nearby towns of Cashel and Callan, instructing the officers in charge to send detachments to Ballingarry and to make sure that both detachments arrived at the same time. However, the men from Callan marched faster and on arrival were attacked by the rebels. The police barricaded themselves in a cottage surrounded by a cabbage patch and beat off all attacks until the other forces arrived from Cashel. The combined forces of police were sufficient to force the rebels to disperse—another revolt had been quelled.

Fifteen years later another revolutionary movement called the Fenians organized a general uprising to take place on 5 March, 1867. The police heard about it and by immediate and stern measures defeated the attempt completely. The British Government were so pleased with the police that they decided that they should in future be called the *Royal* Irish Constabulary and gave £2000 to be divided amongst them as a material reward. They wore a dark green—nearly black— uniform and were armed with carbines and revolvers. They had an intimate knowledge of the countryside and of the people and were, indeed, a most thorough and effective intelligence force.

About the beginning of this century 11,000 of these men policed Ireland. Ireland is a small country and in the various counties many people are related to each other. The police were so organized that they never served as policemen in their own counties, and in a country where county loyalty is very strong a group of policemen from the same county never served in the same police barracks. In the average police barracks in Ireland, therefore, there would be a police sergeant and six constables—each of them from a different county. In this way family and county loyalties were eliminated so that the policemen could concentrate on their work of watching and noting. Every occurrence, no matter how trivial, was noted in what was called the "Day Book" and this book was carefully examined by the various police inspectors on their frequent visits to barracks. They were, for the most part, extremely honest, conscientious men who did not bully nor persecute. I remember one of them who, when he retired, set up as a market gardener. He was extremely just, so just that if you bought 7 lb of potatoes from him he would give exactly 7 lb. If the scales showed a fraction over the 7 lb he would cut a potato in half—and throw the unwanted half away!

In 1910 it seemed very likely that the British Government would grant Ireland "Home Rule", an event to which the Protestants of the North of Ireland strongly objected. Many of these Protestants are the descendants of Scottish people who were given land taken from the native Irish.

From the time of their original settling-in they have regarded the Catholic Irish as their enemies, and the centuries have done little to soften this regard. Superficially it would seem as if they bear a great loyalty to the British Crown, but this is canny hypocrisy. In fact in 1913 a civilian army of Protestant men and women called the Ulster Volunteers smuggled 35,000 rifles and three million rounds of ammunition from Germany to fight against Britain if Britain insisted upon including them in a self-governing Ireland. Their loyalty was, and still is, to their own bigoted principles. They were then led, curiously enough, by a Dublin man, Edward Carson.

It is interesting to note also that Mr Winston Churchill, then First Lord of the Admiralty, ordered part of the English Fleet to anchor off the North of Ireland, and he said that if Belfast fought, his fleet "would have the town in ruins in twenty-four hours".

This gun-running by the Ulster Volunteers led directly to another gun-running, this time by another body of Irish men and women who wanted independence for Ireland—The Irish Volunteers.

It could be described as a very Irish situation, because the chief movers in the gun-running to the South of Ireland were an Englishman, Erskine Childers, helped by Mary Spring-Rice the daughter of an Irish Peer and cousin of the British Ambassador in Washington, a young English Officer named Gordon Shepard, and two fishermen from the West of Ireland.

Erskine Childers, who had once been a clerk in the House of Commons, later an Officer in the British Navy, was to become one of the most successful of the world's propagandists. He bought 1,500 second-hand rifles and 50,000 rounds of ammunition on the Continent and on Sunday 26 July, 1914, the shipment arrived at Howth near Dublin. Mrs Childers was sitting on the yacht that brought the arms, wearing a red pullover—the signal that all was well. A thousand members of the Dublin section of the Irish Volunteers took over the rifles and marched back to Dublin.

The news of the landing had been telephoned to the Dublin Chief of Police, who called out a hundred men of The King's Own Scottish Borderers to seize the rifles. They succeeded in capturing nineteen, and as they marched back to barracks were jeered by a Dublin crowd. When some of the crowd threw stones at the soldiers, the officer ordered his men to halt and make ready to fire. There was a misunderstanding and the soldiers fired. They killed two men and a woman in the crowd and injured thirty-two others.

Subsequently the regiment was known in Ireland as the "King's Own Scottish Murderers". There was an inquiry into the shooting and the Chief of Police, who was not there at all, was dismissed!

In 1914 the First World War started and almost immediately a great controversy started over conscription to the British Army in Ireland. Several thousands of Irishmen joined the British Army and won honours at battle fronts all over the world, but the Irish Nation revolted at the idea of being forced to fight for England. Said a speaker[4] in a Waterford town, "Why in God's name should we fight for the people who are invading us, who remain here only through force of arms, who are trespassing in our country, who have during the past centuries taken the best of our lands and thrown us into hovels, allowed millions of our people to starve, forced more millions to leave their native land in order to eat? They now want us to fight for them—they want us to fight so that they may continue to tyrannize us. Was there ever such stupidity before in the history of Nations!" Michael O'Leary, an Irishman who had won the V.C. fighting the Germans, was sent to Ireland to speak in favour of Irishmen joining the British Army. One day at a recruiting meeting he said, "And you ought to join the army because if the Germans win they will treat us just as bad as the English do." He was withdrawn.

The Royal Irish Constabulary had quelled the Fenian rebellion of 1867, but they had not extinguished it. From it arose a secret society which became known as the Irish Republican Brotherhood, the I R B, whose sworn aim was to defeat the

British and win Ireland's independence. One of their leaders had postulated that "England's difficulty was Ireland's opportunity", and this was well remembered.

This body met in 1914 and decided that the time was right for another armed rebellion against Britain. There was another militant body in Ireland whose sympathies were with those of the I R B. This was the Irish Citizen Army led by James Connolly—an army recruited in the first place to defend the working people from the truncheon attacks of the police. Connolly was a great patriot and his Citizen Army—not a Communist Army—did not always agree with the Irish Volunteers, the political army now being led by the I R B.

Both the Irish Volunteers and the Irish Citizen Army began open drilling and training in arms, watched and noted by the Royal Irish Constabulary. The police were building up a dossier of every name and a knowledge of every face of the men who were training for their next trial of strength with England.

Sir Roger Casement, a valuable servant of the British Government, had become a rabid Irish Nationalist and a member of the Irish Volunteers. He undertook to go to Germany—then at war with Britain—and negotiate with the Germans for arms and artillery. The I R B had very little faith in him and sent their own representative to make arrangements as well. The I R B now decided that Easter week of 1916 should be the time of organized rebellion in Ireland and the Germans were informed of this. The I R B agent, Robert Monteith, accepted an offer from the Germans of 20,000 old Russian rifles, and when Casement heard this he was shocked at its inadequacy. He was convinced that up-to-date small arms, machine-guns, artillery and even a German expeditionary force were necessary if the Irish rebellion was to be successful, but there was little he could do about it in Germany. He returned to Ireland in a German submarine and was arrested by the Royal Irish Constabulary soon after he landed there. He was tried as a traitor and hanged in London.

James Connolly with his 200 men and women of the Irish Citizen Army was anxious to begin the rebellion. The I R B had not taken him into their confidence and were planning for 10,000 armed Irish Volunteers to revolt simultaneously all over Ireland. Anxious that the enthusiastic Connolly should not "shoot the gun", the I R B at length kidnapped him and held him for two days during which time they convinced him to wait until they were ready.

There was another complication. The head of the Irish Volunteers was Eoin MacNeill, who did not believe in armed rebellion and had been elected to the post to mislead the British. The members of the I R B who were planning the rebellion did not tell him their plans, but he heard about the imminent rebellion accidentally and immediately sent out an order to the Volunteers that "all orders issued by Commandant Pearse are hereby cancelled". This was on the Thursday before Easter Monday. Pearse and his colleagues then went to Mac-Neill and told him everything, including the news that a ship full of German arms was due at any moment. They persuaded MacNeill to countermand the instruction he had sent out.

On Good Friday, 1916, the German ship loaded with arms and ammunition arrived off the coast of Kerry where she was seen by a British warship and ordered to steam into the Irish harbour of Queenstown. The German captain at once blew up his ship.

When this news reached MacNeill in Dublin he immediately sent out new orders countermanding the orders he had sent out countermanding his original orders!

He also issued a notice in the Sunday papers ordering every

volunteer not to march at Easter. The leaders of the Rebellion were at their wits' end. Here were months of planning and years of waiting being nullified by their own nominal leader. They decided to go ahead with their plans though they now knew that they could not have the forces they had originally planned to use.

The leaders of the rebels were Patrick Pearse, a schoolmaster, poet and idealist; James Connolly, from the North of Ireland, who had spent twenty years in Scotland and seven in America and returned to Ireland to help found the Irish Socialist Republic Party—a man of action and a revolutionary against all Capitalism, not only British Capitalism; Joseph Plunkett, who was in charge of military operations and had left hospital where he was being treated for tuberculosis; Tom MacDonagh, leader of the Dublin Brigade of the Irish Volunteers; Eamonn Kent; an old Fenian who kept a cigarette shop in Dublin, named Tom Clarke; and Sean McDermott, onetime barman and tram driver, a lame, gay and popular man.

The rebels took over several buildings in the City of Dublin. Patrick Pearse, who was Commandant-General of the Irish Republican Army, read a proclamation from the steps of the General Post Office which declared the setting up of the Provisional Government of the Irish Republic. This document was signed by the seven leaders. Written by Pearse, it began poetically: "In the name of God and dead Generations from which she receives her old traditions of nationhood, Ireland, through us, summons her children to her flag and strikes for her freedom. . . ."

But just then most of the Irish people were not very interested. The men, over 600 of them, barricaded themselves in and waited for the British to move; the police returned to barracks. The denizens of the Dublin slums came into the shopping centres, broke windows and looted—one shameless hussy trying on dress after dress on the sidewalk, another whose bundle of loot had been stolen declaring: "Yez are a lot of thieving bastards to steal me stuff when me back is turned."

The British authorities in Dublin had been taken completely by surprise, there had been no informers. "Informer" is a word that is detested and feared in Ireland, perhaps more than in any other country in the world.

There is an old and completely false tradition in Ireland that informers were responsible for the failure of every previous Irish revolt. In fact, the history of Ireland reveals a few informers only, and those unfortunate creatures never betrayed anything of much importance. Previous Irish rebellions like this one failed through incompetence and bungling by the rebels themselves. It was part of British policy to keep the myth of the informer alive, to make the people believe that they could not trust each other, in order to prevent them from forming underground movements. It is a myth that still exists, one that is a long time dying.

The British found out about the rebellion when twenty armed I R A tried to capture Dublin Castle, the Headquarters of the British Government in Dublin. The rebels bungled the attempt and through poor intelligence lost the most important fortress available to them. A British sentry fired a blank into the air and the guard turned out—they too had blank ammunition and were the only troops guarding the Castle. The rebels withdrew after shooting an unarmed policeman who had defied them.

It being Easter, the British authorities in Dublin and London were taking the week-end off. A young man named Duff Cooper—afterwards to become very famous—decoded telegrams from Dublin but did not attach much importance to them. Lord Wimborne, the British Viceroy in Dublin, had about 2,000 troops available in various Dublin barracks. These were turned out and he also sent to Belfast and the military centre in the Curragh of Kildare about fifty miles away, for reinforcements.

One of the buildings occupied was Boland's flour mill and in charge of it was an unknown young man of thirty-three named Eamonn de Valera, then adjutant of the Dublin Brigade—a bespectacled, lean, tousled-headed schoolteacher. He proved himself the most successful of all the leaders, inflicting heavy casualties on the British troops and being the last commander to surrender.

There was another young man with the I R A in the General Post Office, and he was a very cross young man indeed. He was absolutely furious and deeply shocked by the incompetence of it all. He was working with all his heart and quite prepared to die with his companions, but he was not in the confidence of the leaders and was aghast at the bungling manner in which the rebellion had been organized and was now being prosecuted. His name was Michael Collins.

Wimborne, British Lord Lieutenant of Ireland, issued a proclamation:

"Whereas an attempt, instigated and designed by the foreign enemies of our King and Country to incite rebellion in Ireland and thus endanger the safety of the United Kingdom has been made by a reckless though small body of men who have been guilty of insurrectionary action in the City of Dublin;

"We Ivor Churchill do hereby warn all His Majesty's subjects that the sternest measures are being and will be taken for the prompt suppression of the existing disturbances and the restoration of order:

"And we do hereby enjoin all loyal and law-abiding citizens to abstain from acts or conduct which might interfere with the action of the Executive Government and, in particular, we warn all citizens of the danger of unnecessarily frequenting the streets or public places or of assembling in crowds.

"Given under our seal on the 24th day of April 1916.

"WIMBORNE."

Badly led, poorly equipped and insufficiently trained as the rebels were, they gave an excellent account of themselves and there were many fierce and bitterly fought battles. At the Four Courts, which is the Law Courts of Dublin, a body of volunteers—who called themselves Sinn Feiners ("shinners" to the British)—found only one policeman in charge when they arrived at the building. He handed over the keys and the rebels searched the building, finding a terrified caretaker hiding in the basement. He was reassured and allowed to leave with his belongings.[5]

In this part of Dublin the fighting was particularly bitter. In an area which could be contained within a circle with a diameter of fifty yards the Sinn Feiners and military fired point-blank at each other.

Within the Four Courts rooms were allocated as first-aid posts and beds were commandeered from a nearby hotel. Barricades made of barrels, lorries and upturned carts, reinforced with sacks of meal and bran from bakeries, were erected in the streets, and in front of them was thrown glass from broken bottles.

The first British seen were a party of cavalry escorting a horse-drawn van of ammunition to barracks. A civilian warned the officer in charge that the Sinn Feiners were infesting the area towards which he was going. The officer ignored the warning.

As they came in sight of the Four Courts they were fired on by the rebels and taken completely by surprise. Several of the

soldiers and horses fell, some of the terrified horses stampeded.
A few of the Lancers hopelessly charged the building, and
were shot down. The rest of the horses and men took shelter
in a side street where they remained for four days. The horses
became frantic with hunger and thirst and when the soldiers
released them they continued to run about the streets—the
sound of their hoofs in the night time adding to the eerie horror
and causing many false alarms amongst the rebels.

The rebels took one of the lances dropped by the soldiers
and, tying a Sinn Fein tricolour of green, white and yellow to it,
stuck it in the ground in front of a public house which they
had occupied. The house was kept by a man named Riley and
it subsequently became known as "Riley's Fort".

On Monday night another party of soldiers approached to
within a few hundred feet of the Four Courts. They were
fired upon and several dropped. The rest retired and the rebels
collected five rifles and one thousand rounds of badly needed
ammunition.

On Tuesday, Lord Dunsany the poet-peer drove into the
area with a friend—a British officer in uniform. Called upon
to halt, their driver ignored the order and the rebel fired wounding Lord Dunsany in the cheek and his driver in the hand.
Very shaken indeed and in great trepidation, the three men
were taken in front of the rebel captain, who was himself a
lover of poetry and remembered some of Dunsany's lines.
Using one of them, he said: "You are not yet for the 'Glittering
Gates'," and released them. On his way to the hospital, it is
said, Lord Dunsany congratulated himself on being captured
by some "literary men".

On the Wednesday the I R A searched police barracks at
the rear of the Four Courts and, to their surprise, found
twenty-four policemen and a prisoner being held in custody for

a civil offence, hiding in a coal cellar. They were armed with revolvers and truncheons which were taken from them, and were nearly overcome with fear, hunger and fatigue. They were fed and allowed to leave.

It was reported to the rebels in Riley's Fort that there were soldiers hiding in a nearby barracks. A party of I R A surrounded the building and ordered the soldiers to come out, but they refused to answer. Gelignite was thrust into the wall and exploded to make a breach, and the front door was smashed down with a sledge hammer. Then the military displayed a small white flag and forty unarmed soldiers of the Royal Army Pay Corps marched out, followed by an unarmed policeman. These prisoners were fed and put to work filling sandbags and building barricades.

A number of prisoners including officers and men were now lodged in rooms in the Four Courts. They were treated well and given even more food than the rebels themselves shared. The officers were placed by themselves and supplied with cigarettes and whisky. Some of these officers subsequently repaid this kindness by identifying the rebels and getting them long terms of imprisonment.

On Tuesday many of the residents of the area fully realized that they were in the centre of a battlefield. Some of them refused to leave their homes and paid for their temerity with their lives, but the majority of men, women and children moved out to temporary billets in workhouses and institutions in a healthier part of the city.

The rebels set fire to the empty barracks where they had captured men of the Royal Army Pay Corps. This fire got out of control, spread to other buildings and burned for three days. The nights became like day. A drug warehouse was involved in the flames and barrels of oil exploded at intervals, shooting burning liquid high into the air and over nearby buildings.

On Thursday the military began hand-to-hand attacks on the rebels. First a file of twenty soldiers with bayonets gleaming approached in single file. The rebels held their fire until the soldiers had walked into an area where they came under view of several detachments of the I R A. At a signal a devastating volley exploded and most of the soldiers were hit. An ambulance drove up and the dead bodies and wounded were loaded in and driven off.

The military authorities now began to realize that they were fighting something more than an unruly mob of armed scoundrels and adopted more warlike tactics. (In another part of the city a British officer marched his men in fours into a heavily defended position where they were mown down like ninepins.)

Firing from behind cover the British now began to cause casualties amongst the Sinn Feiners, and priests and doctors appeared on the scene. Military in armoured cars drove into the area; the cars would stop suddenly, and under a covering fire from the mounted machine-guns, the soldiers would drop off and dash into houses. Whilst advancing, the armoured car fired indiscriminately into every house, and residents still living there hid themselves in the cellars or lay flat on the floor.

As the soldiers stormed the houses many of them were shot down—one soldier lifted his rifle to break down a door, and the rifle went off and killed his companion. Once inside a house the soldiers broke down walls into the houses next door, and they approached nearer and nearer to the positions held by the rebels.

During this period, the soldiers, now thoroughly incensed, shot everybody and anybody whom they came across in the houses they were passing through. On Friday evening the firing from the British had become so heavy that the rebels decided to move the prisoners to another building for safety. They were shepherded under heavy fire. The bullets spattered the wall around the party who stumbled in the dusk over the barricades and obstacles. The fire power from the machine-guns of the armoured cars was terrific, searchlights played on bullet-spattered streets and hand grenades burst incessantly.

None of the prisoners was injured, but two of the guards were wounded. In their new prison the captured men were made as comfortable as possible and given cigarettes. Many of them were soldiers who had but recently returned from the battlefields of France, and they took a philosophic and pro-fessional interest in their plight. They explained to their captors the various and to them familiar sounds of rifle fire, auto-matic weapons, machine-guns, and light and heavy artillery, which were now creating a hideous cacophony. The single shot rifles which had been landed at Howth were being used by the rebels and their dull boom easily distinguished them and gave away the position of their owners.

The rebels were now jealously hoarding the little ammuni-tion they had left and fired only when essential. This misled the officers in charge of the military and early on Saturday they ordered another bayonet charge on the rebel positions. The troops met a withering fire and retreated, leaving many of their number lying on the ground. The rebels ran out to pick up the fallen rifles and collected all the ammunition they could find. Most of the rifles, however, had been shattered by their own bullets. Late on Friday, men of the Staffordshire regiment and the Sherwood Foresters took up positions about the rebel strongholds. On Saturday, before dawn, the bombardment and counter-firing subsided.

It was only a short pause, however, and soon it had redoubled its fury. The main attack of the military was concentrated on Riley's Fort, now defended by eight completely exhausted, hungry and sleep-starved men. Jack Shouldice was in charge—a man of cool and determined character who had been slipping from position to position during the night.

He ordered Patrick O'Flanagan to go to a nearby barricade for hand grenades. Ignoring the bullets which swept the street, O'Flanagan ran across and obtained them. Coming back he appeared to trip slightly in the middle of the road, but the impetus of his rush carried him on through Riley's doorway—he had been fatally wounded and died within a few minutes.

Riley's Fort now became untenable. The small garrison made a rush for it and safely reached another house nearby. The soldiers had occupied the Fort. Later the rebels—about sixty of them—decided to try and recapture it from the military, but this party was outflanked by the military and held stationary by small-arms fire.

The position of the British in the Fort was now in jeopardy, however, and a large body of military set out to relieve them. A civilian resident still clinging to the shaky security of his own house was a very unwilling observer of the fight at this stage. He described it as "perfectly infernal", for the soldiers and rebels were only a few yards apart and sometimes in adjoining doorways. Several soldiers fell, but a body of them gained possession of a bakery opposite the Fort. A sergeant-major and some other soldiers were killed and in the height of the conflict one young British soldier fell wounded in full view of both sides. There was a lull in the firing whilst two ambulance men went in and removed him.

A nearby hall, called Father Mathew Hall, was being used as a casualty station and was crowded with wounded and dying of both sides as well as by wounded civilians. The supply of drugs and surgical appliances was running out and a Catholic priest, Father Augustine, hearing this, sent a rebel Red Cross man to the military commander to ask for a brief interval to move the injured to hospital.

After an hour's absence the messenger returned and stated that the British officers had held a conference and given him a verbal message to bring back. It was: "You are all rebels and you will get none of the amenities of war"—a nice turn of phrase.

Father Augustine and his colleague Father Aloysius then went through the firing to the military, where they met a Lieutenant-Colonel Taylor. They were accompanied by the same Red Cross man.

The group met in the street and decided to send the Red Cross man to the rebel leader—Patrick Holohan—to discuss the matter. Just then a splatter of bullets struck the pavement near where they were standing. The British officer wheeled around and covered the Red Cross man with his revolver. Father Augustine intervened, the officer cooled down, and the priest offered to go himself.

He made his way openly and defencelessly through the bullet-scourged streets and, standing outside the house which the rebels were defending, called out his message through the windows for Patrick Holohan. Holohan's reply was that, speaking for himself and the men under him, he would not make any terms with the military, but if the Fathers of the Church considered it necessary he would agree to a temporary truce for the removal of the wounded.

Father Augustine returned to the British officer and a temporary truce was agreed. It was to last from 7.30 p.m. on Saturday until 10 a.m. on Monday.

The conduct of the priests during the Dublin rebellion was above all praise. They ignored all danger in their work of succouring the wounded without any reference to which side the injured belonged. One Franciscan whose church was in the centre of the battle was told that a rebel was dangerously wounded and should be taken to hospital immediately. With a Dr D. Flanagan, he walked across a street covered by an intense cross-fire. The doctor and the priest put the wounded man on a stretcher and somebody threw a Red Cross flag across the priest's shoulders. The two men then carried the stretcher safely through flying bullets to hospital. The Red Cross was not always so respected—one flag thrust through a window in Moore Street was riddled the moment it appeared.

In the meantime the General Post Office, the Headquarters of the I R A, had been shelled and set on fire. The rebels left the building and moved into a row of nearby houses, but it became clear that the end had been reached and that further resistance could only lead to more unnecessary deaths.

Nurses had been in the G.P.O. all the week with the I R A and when it was evacuated most of them had been sent out under a Red Cross flag. Three of them remained. Patrick Pearse sent for one of them, Elizabeth O'Farrell, and asked her to take a message to the officer commanding the military: it was that the Commandant-General of the I R A wished to negotiate with the Commandant-General of the British forces in Ireland.

She was politely received by Brigadier-General Lowe, officer in charge of military operations in Dublin, but he would have nothing to do with conditional surrender and sent a message back through her, that the rebels must surrender unconditionally. On Saturday, at 3 p.m. they did.

Pearse sent the following message by Miss O'Farrell to the leaders of the rebel strongholds in Dublin: "In order to prevent the further slaughter of Dublin citizens and in the hope of saving the lives of our followers the members of the provisional

Government present at Headquarters have agreed to an unconditional surrender and the Commandants of the various districts in the city and country will order their commands to lay down arms."

This order was handed to Patrick Holohan, in charge of the party in the Four Courts area, and after consultation with his men he hung out a white flag. Outside Riley's Fort the remnants of his men lined up and, in the presence of the military, Holohan told his men: "Fellow soldiers of the Irish Republican Army, I have just received a communication from Commandant Pearse calling on us to surrender, and you will agree with me that this is the hardest part that we have been called upon to perform during this eventful week, but we came into this fight for Irish independence in obedience to the commands of our higher officers and now in obedience with their wishes we must surrender. I know you would, like myself, prefer to be with our comrades who have already fallen in the fight—we, too, should rather die in this glorious struggle than submit to the enemy. The treatment you may expect in the future you may judge from the past."

He ordered his fifty-eight remaining men to turn right and they marched under military guard to Dublin Castle.

Jack Shouldice, now a fit elderly widower, fondled the five-chambered Smith and Wesson revolver which he still keeps as a souvenir as he told me: "I remember building the barricades around Riley's Fort. We seized everything portable, except necessary articles of furniture, from the houses around, stores, shops and back yards. The barricades consisted of broken furniture, cases, full and empty barrels, some of them full of paraffin oil which was dangerous, but it was all we could get, a hackney cab, carts without wheels and sacks of flour and meal. The owner of the hackney cab came along later with a dilapidated old cart and begged me to let him swop it for the hackney cab which was his only means of livelihood—we had to agree. Then another resident begged us to remove a full barrel of oil from his house, which we did—we put it in the middle of the road and later it was peppered with bullets. Later we reinforced the barricades with rubble, sand, and planks from a builder's yard. We barricaded Riley's and broke holes in the walls into the adjoining houses.

"All the police had been withdrawn from the streets and most of the bakeries in the city had stopped working. There was a bakery in our area, but the officer, Commandant Daly, would not allow it to stop work. Hundreds of people from all over the city came to the bakery for bread and we had to regulate the queues. It wasn't easy at first and we got a great deal of abuse from the citizens for the trouble we were causing—later on though they took a better view of us.

"At the beginning of the week it was mostly sniping at each other from elevated positions and they certainly had some good shots. My brother Frank who was with me was sniping through a small slit when somebody in the room called him. As he turned his head a bullet grazed his cheek.

"On Monday and Tuesday a good number of local residents, especially those who had relatives fighting with the British Army against the Germans, were very antagonistic and their womenfolk especially were very abusive. We gradually got their sympathy when they saw we were conducting ourselves well and fighting a clean fight against much superior forces.

"On Monday evening we had a very busy time with people coming from the races and back from Easter holidays. They were mostly in a state of panic and anxious to get to their homes, some of them were obstreperous, but they soon stopped arguing when they realized we were in deadly earnest.

"Later in the week the military started approaching us by breaking through house after house. They murdered fourteen or fifteen civilians mostly in North King Street during this period. On the Monday a friend of mine who lived there, Peadar Lawless, passed through the barriers on his way to play football. He was not in the movement. Half jokingly I held him up and asked him if he would like to join us. I said I could get him a rifle. He replied that he was not in the movement and that it was a bit late to join now. He passed on—he was one of the fellows murdered later on by the military.

"It was very tough on the Saturday through deaths, wounds and illness and after two days of continuous defence fighting without sleep. We were only eight—wearied out and stupefied from lack of sleep. Later that day we heard that there was to be a conditional surrender, but afterwards we were told it was to be unconditional. This put us into a very depressed state, knowing what to expect from our old enemy. Nevertheless, we had a feeling of pride for having defied them with all their power for a week."

One hundred and three British officers and men were killed during the week, 357 wounded and nine missing; fourteen members of the Royal Irish Constabulary were killed and twenty-three wounded, and three members of the Dublin Metropolitan Police were killed and three wounded. Fifty-two Sinn Feiners were killed in action, 450 civilians were killed and 2,614 were wounded.

One rather frightful incident which gave a foretaste of the terror to come was the murder of Francis Sheehy-Skeffington and two Dublin journalists. Sheehy-Skeffington was a well-known Dublin eccentric—a pacifist, humanitarian and a supporter of the Suffragettes. He was arrested by a British officer during the week and lodged in military barracks from which he would in the normal way have been released within a few hours. Unfortunately one Captain J. C. Bowen-Colthurst decided that the oddly dressed little man with a Suffragette badge in his buttonhole was dangerous. Later this officer arrested two Dublin journalists, Thomas Dickson and Patrick McIntyre—neither of them a member of the I R A. Bowen-Colthurst had the three men taken into the barrack yard and executed by a firing squad. He was later charged with murder, found to be insane, and sent to a criminal lunatic asylum to be detained "during His Majesty's pleasure". His plea was that he thought they might escape. Incidents like this—and the same excuse—became dreadfully familiar in Ireland in the years that followed.

James Kenny[6] was a volunteer in Patrick Pearse's own Battalion, the 4th. As a special privilege "E" Company of this Battalion had been allotted a place in the occupation and defence of the rebel Headquarters, the G P O.

On the morning of the Rebellion James Kenny with the rest of "E" Company met at Rathfarnum Church and were ordered to march to Liberty Hall. As they were forming into line Eoin McNeill, the President, who had issued instructions against the mobilization, met them and told them to go home as the rebellion had been cancelled. The officer in charge of the Company politely replied: "We have had our orders—we are going in."

Proud of the fact that they had been chosen for Headquarters and looking upon themselves as the personal bodyguard of Commandant-General Pearse, the Company, well armed and well led, reached Liberty Hall and were directed to the G P O.

They prepared themselves there for the defence and whilst doing so were joined by two sailors, one a Norwegian, the other a Dutchman. These two were ordered off the premises but they said they had come to fight with the I R A. They boasted that they knew all about guns and that it was their wish to "fight on the side of the small nationalities".

The I R A agreed that they could remain and James Kenny handed the Dutch sailor a loaded double-barrelled shot gun. The "expert" immediately managed to fire it accidentally and a charge of buck shot rebounded off the wall and entered Kenny's foot—probably the first casualty of the rebellion. Kenny's foot was cleaned and bandaged by Dr Jim Ryan and he carried on all right for the rest of the week.

On the Saturday Kenny ran from the burning building beside the stretcher on which the many-times wounded James Connolly was being carried. They crossed the road into Moore Lane and Connolly ordered one of his men to break down the door leading into a bottle store. The man raised his rifle to obey, touched the trigger and shot himself dead

They were continually under fire from a British machine-gun at the end of Moore Street. An order reached them that all men with bayonets were to report to the O C. Kenny did not possess a bayonet, neither did his friend Paddy Sweeny, but Paddy's brother Jim did have one and Jim started to move off. "Come on," said Paddy to Kenny. "We can't—we have no bayonets," Kenny replied. "I'm going, anyway—if I don't, who will look after Jim?" said Paddy. The order, however, was cancelled. Pearse had decided to attempt a bayonet attack on the machine-gun post but changed his mind because there were still some women in the party. Pearse's decision in this case was humanitarian, just as his final decision to surrender was. He said after his capture, "I saw soldiers shooting civilians and children deliberately—it could not go on, we had to give in."

3

AFTER THE SURRENDER

As the prisoners surrendered on Saturday afternoon they were marched under strong military guards to the Rotunda hospital where they were herded together in the open behind tall railings and left there until Sunday morning, some wounded, all exhausted. And here an Irishman, Captain Lee Wilson, had "fun" with the captured rebels[1]. He had prisoners stripped and he slashed at them with his bamboo cane. He tortured Tom Clarke, the old Fenian. Tom was well known in Dublin to the police and everybody else.

That night police went amongst the prisoners picking out the leaders. They avoided Tom Clarke, until one R I C man arrived and immediately picked him out. Standing nearby was the angry young man of the G P O. He had distinguished himself that week. His rank was that of Staff Captain and he was described as the most efficient officer in the building. It was Collins who led the final desperate charge from the burning Headquarters. Now he watched Tom Clarke being identified by an officious and revenge-hungry policeman. "We'll be back for him," he said. That night both Lee Wilson and the R I C man sealed their own fates: both were shot by the I R A afterwards.

Next morning the prisoners were marched through the ruins of Dublin's main street—still littered with the bodies of civilians and horses—to military barracks where they were carefully scrutinized and divided into batches. Everything they possessed was taken from them and never returned. The "G" men, the detective force of the Dublin Metropolitan police, were busiest in picking out the leaders.

"The real black sheep were placed on one side of the hall, including me," said Jack Shouldice, "and we were kept for court martial. The main body of the prisoners were sent by boat that night to concentration camps in Britain. We were before the court martial singly or in pairs during the week. During that period we had to rest on the bare floors of our cells and sleep as best we could. The trials were a farce. A young British soldier who was a prisoner in the G P O swore that he saw Con O'Donovan and myself—we were tried together—in the active fighting in the G P O. Neither of us were in the G P O at all during the week.

"The 'G' men were for all practical purposes the Judge and Jury—they were present throughout all the trials, identified us for the army officer holding the court martial, and gave them our character and our records. Most of these 'G' men paid for their help with their lives afterwards. O'Donovan and myself were taken to Kilmainham gaol on the following Friday and were put into the cells of Mallin and Kent on the third floor—they had been taken down to the ground floor for execution. For a few days we were left alone expecting to be taken out and shot the same as the others. We could hear the shots of the firing squad every morning as they executed the leaders in twos and threes. Then on Tuesday an officer came to the cells and read us our sentences. Mine was 'sentenced to death' . . . the officer paused . . . 'but the officer presiding at the court martial has commuted the sentence to five years penal servitude.'

"We were taken to Mountjoy prison where for the first time for a fortnight we had what we considered to be real comfort—

a bath, a bunk and some food, even though it was prison food. The warders were, generally speaking, humane—unlike the soldiers, though even some of the soldiers were all right if you had a shilling or two to bribe them.

"After a week in Mountjoy, a dozen of us, including de Valera (he too had been sentenced to death but because of his American citizenship this sentence had been commuted to imprisonment), Harry Boland, Jack MacArdle, Dick King, Michael de Lacey, Seamus Rafter, Con O'Donovan, Frank Lawless and Jim O'Sullivan were marched to a cargo vessel and we sailed to England. We were imprisoned in Dartmoor prison."

Shortly afterwards, they were joined by another prisoner, Eoin MacNeill, the man whose orders and counter-orders had bedevilled the battle plans of the Irish Republicans on the eve of the Easter rising. Understandably there was a "feeling" against this man. He had been responsible for stopping simultaneous risings throughout the whole of Ireland and for 600 instead of 2,000 rebels appearing on the streets of Dublin.

His first appearance was on the morning after his arrival. The other Irish prisoners were lined up under the supervision of the warders when MacNeill—still the nominal Chief of the Irish Volunteer movement—appeared and walked to take his place. De Valera stepped out from his ranks and gave the order: "Irish Volunteers—Attention—Eyes Left."

This gesture of de Valera's and the salute accorded by the prisoners acknowledged the sincerity and integrity of Mac-Neill's intentions, and though his part as the "cover" for I R B was now finished it re-established him in the regard of rank and file of the I R A.

De Valera was severely cautioned by the Governor for his breach of prison discipline but the warning had little effect and he continued to be a most intractable prisoner. He was subsequently transferred to Maidstone prison after an incident in which he threw a loaf of black bread which he could not stomach across to Jack McArdle who was prepared to eat it. The loaf did not find its mark and was picked up by the Chief Warder, who reported the matter.

Michael Collins was not sent to Dartmoor. He too, though unknown to the authorities, had been picked out as "dangerous" in the identity parade at Richmond barracks in Dublin, and he had been sent to line up against the wall with the others for court martial.

As he stood there exhausted and depressed but still alert he heard his name being called out from a different part of the hall. He looked up and tried to make out who was calling him. He could not tell. Again his name was called out and he still could not identify the speaker. A third time he heard his name, and this time he made his mind up and strode across the hall to where the not-so-dangerous prisoners were gathered. Nobody stopped him. Thus, inexplicably, the man who afterwards beat single-handedly the armed and diplomatic power of Britain escaped from their clutches.

Single-handedly? They tell the story in Dublin of an American who boasted that the largest building in the world was in New York. A Dublin man protested that Dublin had it and when the American asked the proof the Dubliner led him to O'Connell Street and, pointing to the G P O, said: "According to the stories you hear in Ireland, that building held a million and a half men during the Irish Rebellion of 1916."

Collins was the greatest man thrown up by Ireland since Ireland was first invaded by the British in 1172. Collins once said: "All I want to lead is sixty determined trustworthy men, and I'll beat the British." Collins used little more than sixty men in his subsequent campaign—a campaign which was the greatest bluff in history, a campaign which was conceived, organized and prosecuted to the bitter end by Collins in spite of, rather than with the help of, his colleagues.

But now on 30 April, 1916, Collins was on his way with 238 other prisoners to detention barracks in Stafford, England, and from there to an internment camp in Frongoch in Wales.

The Irish people were gravely disturbed by the rebellion. In a Waterford village, Tallow, the people cheered when the local police sergeant read out a telegram which stated that the rebels had been crushed, and this cheering was echoed throughout the land. The relatives of hundreds of thousands of Irishmen who were fighting in British regiments in France were particularly bitter against the Sinn Feiners. The rebels had achieved nothing by their hopeless blood-soaked gesture. But the British had come to the rescue!

They shot the rebel leaders—not quickly and humanely, but in batches of twos and threes. Morning after morning for a week the rebels were led out and executed. James Connolly could not walk so they wheeled him out and shot him. The shots of the execution squads now echoed throughout the length and breadth of Ireland and the cheers for the British were choked.

General Maxwell, soon to be known as "Bloody" Maxwell, was in charge of the military. The sentences of death on fourteen of the leaders, including all the men who signed the Proclamation of the Provisional Government of the Irish Republic, were confirmed and carried out. So died Patrick Pearse and his brother Willie, MacDonagh, old Tom Clarke, Plunkett, MacDermott, Connolly, Eamonn Kent, Edward Daly who was in charge of the Four Courts area, Heuston, MacBride, O'Hanrahan, Mallin and Colbert. Thomas Kent was executed for killing a sergeant of the R I C in Co. Cork on the Tuesday of Easter Week.

The shooting of Willie Pearse is the least understandable, but Willie welcomed it. He was shot not because he was one of the leaders—he was only one of the rank and file—but because he was the brother of Patrick—and Willie shrunk at the idea of going home alone to his mother.

For eight months the Irish prisoners remained in their internment camps—valuable months of thinking and planning. Especially valuable to Collins, who had seen the results of bad planning and poor organization. He wrote from Frongoch: "They have died nobly at the hands of firing squads. So much I grant. But I do not think the Rising week was an appropriate time for the issue of a memorandum couched in poetic phrase nor of actions worked out in a similar fashion. Looking at it from the inside (I was in the G P O) it had the air of a Greek tragedy about it, the illusion being more or less completed with the issue of the before-mentioned memorandum. Of Pearse and Connolly, I admire the latter the most. Connolly was a realist, Pearse the direct opposite. . . . On the whole, I think the Rising was bungled terribly, costing many a good life. It seemed at first to be well organized but afterwards became subjected to panic decisions and a great lack of every essential organization and co-operation."

At Frongoch Collins emerged as a shrewd and determined organizer. The prisoners claimed political status and refused to be treated as criminal prisoners. They made their points in many ways and suffered many deprivations of privileges. The leader of these demonstrations was Collins and the success of the demonstrations was due to his intelligent handling and organization.

Already his genius, his enormous capacity for cool-headed

appraisal of any situation and his amazing gift of influencing and winning the confidence of men were apparent. He was an I R B man and ideals of the Brotherhood were deeply ingrained in his soul. Prison was an incident, an incident which should be used for the furtherance of his convictions. This robust, shrewd peasant leader was even now planning the fate of his peasant race.

The poets and the dreamers had been banished by the firing squads of the British. Now, still a junior officer in the Movement, Collins began his inevitable progress towards a position where he could wield the impersonal, unyielding, completely ruthless campaign which would confuse the power of the British Empire and render its overwhelming superiority in men and arms its greatest weakness against Ireland.

Lesser men believed in the power of the gun to defeat Britain and some men today believe that this actually happened. Collins knew the fatuity of such nonsense, not that he ever troubled much to explain it. Collins was self-sufficient, he knew the gun to be but a propaganda weapon, its power of destruction a headline, its detonation a slogan. He had no intention of challenging the might of an Empire. He was determined to challenge its weakness.

At Christmas 1916 Collins and the rest of the prisoners were released and returned to meet a tumultous reception from the people of Ireland, many of whom had booed them eight months before.

In 1917 Collins, who had been working full time with the organization, was appointed Director of Organization of the Irish Volunteers, and de Valera was elected President. Collins drafted a new constitution for the Volunteers, one which pinpointed him as an organizer of exceptional ability.

The following year Britain, who wanted to enforce conscription in Ireland because of lack of manpower on the Western front, faced a completely united Ireland which rejected the proposals, and early in 1918 the British falsely alleging a German plot in Ireland, arrested all the Sinn Fein leaders and lodged them once more in English gaols. Collins avoided arrest and became a wanted man.

Following the enforced absence of the other leaders, much of the organization and running of the movement devolved upon Collins and it was from that date that the real organization came into being.

Many men of the I R A had trained in the British Army and were well acquainted with the use of arms and explosives. Apart from some hurried pre-rebellion training, Collins knew little about arms or explosives; he had never had military training; he should not have known anything about the way in which chiefs think and operate; yet as Director of Organization he built up a civilian army, a small, poorly armed force, that badgered and goaded into reprisal fully-trained and heavily armed troops and police.

He appreciated the vital importance of intelligence, both to the enemy and to himself, and in 1918 he began to build his own intelligence service. This was not, in fact, his province. The Minister of Defence was Cathal Brugha, which is the Irish way of saying Charles Burgess. Cathal, a man of the highest integrity and magnificent principles, had a tidy pigeon-hole type of mind. He did not get on well with Collins and, hearing that Collins had his own intelligence service, he went to him and remonstrated, asking that particulars should be handed over to his department. Collins refused—he said he was not prepared to risk the lives of his agents through bureaucracy.

Nobody knew all Collins's agents except himself, and

because of this some of them subsequently lost their lives. Collins knew his own plan of campaign and he carried it through relentlessly. The other leaders trusted him implicitly but they knew also that they did not know everything Collins was doing. His chief card was intelligence and his only aim was to make it impossible for the British Government to function in Ireland. He knew he could not defeat the British in the field so he fought them in the only possible way. He made the British defeat themselves and anything that stood in the way of his plan was ruthlessly and efficiently annihilated.

Thus it was with the British Intelligence service. When it became dangerous he abolished it with one final gesture—on Bloody Sunday.

[4]

GUERILLA WARFARE

O n 21 January, 1919, came the first killing of members of the
Royal Irish Constabulary. The first two were fifty-six-years-
old Constable MacDonnell, father of seven children, and
Constable O'Connell. MacDonnell was a typical, harmless,
village constable whose great joke was to ask children to spell
rhododendron and then teach them the correct spelling. On
that day they were the escort for a hundredweight and a half of
gelignite which was being sent to a quarry at Soloheadbeg in
Co. Tipperary. As they walked behind the horse and cart
bearing the explosive, eight members of the Irish Republican
Army jumped from behind a wall and called upon them to put
up their hands.

Both the constables went for their carbines and one of the
I R A leaders, Sean Tracey, shot the two of them dead. There
were eight I R A there because they expected a larger police
escort, and they were acting under strict orders not to shoot
unless it was vitally necessary.

One more or less accepts village constables and nobody
likes the idea of shooting them. A legend grew up in Ireland
that these two innocent men were shot dead by a gang of
cowardly I R A from behind the shelter of a wall, and the
majority of the Irish people condemned the shooting as wan-
ton. It was far from that: time and again the R I C proved that
they would not be intimidated by show of arms and the action
of the two policemen in grabbing at their carbines was typical

of the courage of the force. They gave the I R A no alternative but that of shooting and they were not shot by cowardly men.

The men in charge of the ambush were Seamus Robinson, Sean Tracey and Dan Breen—three men who in the succeeding years proved their utter disregard for danger over and over again. Tracey and Breen on a later occasion shot their way out of a house surrounded by military, and Tracey frequently went on one-man raids against groups of police and military.

Immediately after the shooting of the two policemen the county was inundated with military and police searching for the men and the gelignite. One night as the three cases of the explosive were being moved in a horse and cart—the driver sitting on the boxes—police stopped the cart and questioned the driver. The sergeant in charge held up a stick of gelignite which he had found in a field where it had been placed as a decoy by the I R A and asked the driver if he knew what it was. "I think it is a bit of candy," said the driver. "It is not," said the sergeant, "it's a bit of the gelignite that the Sinn Feiners took when they murdered the two policemen." "Oh, if you found that bit you must be near the rest of it," said the driver, who was allowed to drive off[1].

The 11,000 men of the Royal Irish Constabulary now came under a long and bitter attack from the I R A. They were publicly and socially ostracized by the Irish people as were their wives and families. They were attacked in their barracks which they usually bravely defended as long as possible. At Newtown Hamilton, in Co. Antrim, Sergeant Traynor and five constables withstood a four-hour attack[2]. The rebels blew in the gable and set fire to the front of the building, and when the roof fell in the police went into the yard and continued to resist until the rebels retired. The sergeant's wife was with the policemen all the time doing what she could to help.

Coroners' courts upheld the rights of the I R A to shoot policemen. When an I R A man named John Breen shot Sergeant Carroll dead in Milmichael, the sergeant's colleague shot Breen dead. The verdict of the coroner's jury was, "we find that John Breen died of shock and haemorrhage caused by a bullet wound inflicted by Constable Martin whilst John Breen was fighting for his country."[3]

At Bandon, Sergeant Mulhern went to eight o'clock Mass one morning. As he stepped inside the church and was bless- ing himself with holy water he was shot dead. When Con- stable Brett was killed in Cork no undertaker would provide a hearse to take his body to the graveyard.

The police were certainly going through a bad time but this item of news in the *Constabulary Gazette* of December 1920 is—to say the least—puzzling: "The police at Doolin, Co. Clare are suffering terribly from want of food. They have frequently to walk to the village five miles away and have nothing to eat but a few lobsters from the previous day."

The I R A men attacked the police barracks at Ballytrain, in Co. Monaghan, which was defended by six policemen[4]. The police were called upon but refused to surrender, so the I R A blew down the gable of the barracks with a land mine. The police continued to resist until their ammunition had gone. Then the I R A entered. "Why didn't you surrender?" asked the leader. "We had no intention of doing that," said the sergeant, "whilst we had anything left to fight with." One policeman who was wounded was tended by the I R A, who gave him a first-aid pack and some religious symbols. Whilst the I R A were searching the barracks one of the policemen said to them, "There's £60 in that box you are looking at."

"We don't want your money," said the leader, "we came here for arms."

"There is no denying the fact that the number and frequency of police tragedies that have recently occurred are calculated to appal the stoutest heart," said the *Constabulary Gazette* of 3 March, 1920. "No man going forth in the morning can be sure of returning safely. In the hotel, on the roadside, sheltering from the storm, within the barrack walls, leaving the church after Divine Service, it is all the same—callously and in cold blood policemen are being shot down as men shoot game."

Nevertheless the same paper also reflected the spirit of the force when it suggested that police barracks should be fitted with microphones to relieve "the tension on the human ear. These organs give every indication of being overworked at the present time. On some listeners the auricle is so well developed that it projects at an angle of 90 degrees and gives a perceptible forward bend at the slightest sound. Rather funny, isn't it?"

At the same time the young constables were campaigning for the removal of a ban which forbade them from marrying until they had served seven years, and then the lady of their choice had to be vetted by superior authorities—she might be a Sinn Feiner.

One letter about the ban from a member of the force at that time read[5]: ". . . such an unreasonable state of affairs is disgusting especially at the present time when sandbags are congesting all our windows."

In spite of the shootings, intimidation and ostracization, the police continued for a time to try and carry out their civil duties and were inclined to regard the I R A as gangs of scoundrels, who would eventually fade away. The attitude of a large section of the R I C was made clear in a startling way

in the police barracks at Listowel, Co. Kerry, in June 1920.[6]
Lieutenant-Colonel Ferguson Smyth, one-armed Divisional
Commissioner of the police for six counties, addressed
eighteen policemen in this fashion:

"Sinn Fein has had all the sport up to the present and we
are going to have the sport now. I am promised as many troops
from England as I require, thousands are coming daily. I am
also getting 7,000 police from England.

"Police and military will patrol the country at least five
times a week. They are not to confine themselves to the main
roads but take across country, lie in ambush and when
civilians aproach shout 'hands up'. Should the order not be
obeyed shoot and shoot with effect. If persons approaching
carry their hands in their pockets and are in any way suspicious
shoot them down . . . the more you shoot the better I will
like it and I assure you no policeman will get into trouble for
shooting a man. We want your assistance in carrying out this
scheme and wiping out Sinn Fein."

The police stared at him bleakly and wordlessly. "Are you
prepared to co-operate?" he asked. Constable Jeremiah Mee
stood up and said, "By your accent, sir, I take it you are an
Englishman; and in your ignorance you forget you are address-
ing Irishmen." Taking off his cap, revolver and belt he placed
them on the table in front of the Lieutenant-Colonel and
added "these too, are English. Take them."

The local Inspector of police who was present shouted an
order for Mee to be arrested, but his companions stood motion-
less and after a silent, pregnant pause the Lieutenant-Colonel
and his colleagues left the barracks.

A few days later he was sipping whiskey in his club in Cork
city when civilians entered the room, shot him dead and
walked out again.

The news that police were to be recruited in England did not please the R I C, hard pressed though they were. The leader writer in the *Constabulary Gazette* of February 1920 wrote: "Ireland is seeking recruits from the other side. It cannot be done by masters, try as you may," and he launched into an account of the more trivial shortcomings of the Irish policeman's lot. . . . "Seven years before you can marry and then your wife faces an inquisition and now married men are coming into a pallet of straw, a bare and comfortless day room, no armchair, no privacy even in the dormitory . . . and we say nothing about the bomb-throwing fraternity who lie in wait for the policeman confined to barracks. Let that item pass. St Paul is accredited with saying that if a man is married he does well but if a man does not marry he does better. Be it so. Our advice to the Authorities is to let the police constable take the choice. St Paul has a wide knowledge of human nature but he never lived in a police barrack."

But the shootings and resignations from the Constabulary forced the British authorities to find men in England. First the Black and Tans were recruited.

The Black and Tans, we are told *ad nauseam*, were an infamous force, a force of ex-convicts, thieves and murderers that were unleashed and with bloodshot eyes and drooling jaws ravished Ireland, murdering, burning and looting. Many of them earned that reputation, but without them Irish independence would have been lost and all Collins's plans neutralized.

With few exceptions they were ex-soldiers back from a brutalizing war, out-of-work and anxious to get any kind of a job. They were offered good pay as members of the Royal Irish Constabulary and they jumped at it. They were neither better nor worse than other English, Scottish, Welsh or Irish

men of the same age and experience. They were unlucky
enough to be recruited by an overworked and callous government and sent to an area where they became welcomed stooges
of a brilliant enemy. They were well behaved and anxious to
learn when they came first, but that was not what Collins
wanted. They were badly led and badly disciplined, and
within a short time the Black and Tans were tricked into
becoming the best weapons in the impoverished Irish
armoury.

They were despised and ignored by the I R A, who recognized them as much inferior articles, and they were feared
and hated by the unarmed people of Ireland, who came to be
the victims of their senseless and frequently murderous
reprisals. But the people of Ireland had to suffer if the plans
of the I R A were to succeed. It was bad enough when a
column of I R A was not stirring up trouble; it became disastrous when the Black and Tans behaved decently.

The British Government were tricked as well and Lloyd
George played into the hands of Collins time and time again.
He believed as most of the Irish believed that the British
forces were fighting a large army of guerillas, and most of
the Irish people still believe it. To accept this is to under-
estimate the brilliance of the I R A and the genius of Collins.
Those members of the I R A who carried arms and took part
in the fighting war were the cream of fighting men. They were
principalled, courageous, religious and rigorously disciplined,
and they were pathetically few.

The strictly religious training of these men of the I R A
both helped and hindered. In battle for their own country
death was not what they feared most but dishonour. When it
was their business to execute a man they were loth and worried if the man chose to die cursing and swearing, and it was

a relief to most of them when he asked for a clergyman or time to pray.

Newspaper after newspaper of those times reports large gangs of armed I R A attacking barracks; nearly always the rebel force was said to be of 100 to 150 men. Every time the police or military were ambushed it was, according to the same sources, by hundreds of rebels far outnumbering the forces of the Crown. The Government and the people fell for it when a little quiet consideration would have revealed the truth. The I R A had neither the trained men nor the arms to field more than 500 at any one time, and in Dublin City, the hotbed of violence, shootings and explosions, there were rarely more than twenty-five men of the I R A under arms.

To return to the Black and Tans. They arrived knowing nothing about the Irish or their troubles, only knowing that the Irish were an easy-going hospitable race always ready for a drink and a song. They found themselves in a peasant country which had missed the Industrial Revolution and where no middle class existed; they found themselves in a foreign land policing a foreign race who talked English. They, like their masters, made the mistake of thinking it was just another English county. They, like their masters, underestimated the intelligence, the bitter depth of feeling, the patriotism, the courage and, above all, the intentions of the controller of the I R A and the people.

At first because of the shortage of supplies they wore a mixture of khaki uniform and the deep green—nearly black— uniform of the Royal Irish Constabulary. Within a few months they were dressed the same as the R I C and could not be distinguished from them, but the name Black and Tan stuck. (It was coined by a Dublin reporter who first used it in a story to the Press Association.) They were distributed about the country, five or six or more of them joining each station and living and working with the R I C. For the most part the Irishmen did not mix well with the newcomers—in some barracks they were completely ostracized.

I knew one of them, who used to leave his barracks each morning and cross the street to a public house. He carried a revolver in his hand. In the public house he would bolt himself into a little room adjoining the bar—they call these little rooms "snugs" in Ireland—and he would drink himself stupid in a few hours; then he would return to the barracks and sleep it off. He had just left the British Army. He had worked in market gardens in Worthing before the war—when he was very drunk he used to sing "We are the men of Sussex", and so forth, and the Irish people in the public house thought it a nice song. Now and then he would send for a pound of bacon rashers and eat them raw. The Irish people thought this peculiar, but as they used to say: "Sure, 'tis a free country!"

His colleagues were not so peace-loving. One of them, a North of Ireland man, also used to get drunk. One summer afternoon I watched him pull out his bayonet and chase an old man whose son was in the I R A. Fear and the results of alcohol contrived to save the old man, who outran his pursuer.

I watched the same Black and Tan pull out his revolver one day, stop a young draper's assistant and march him into the police barracks. A few minutes afterwards we heard a shot. Then the young draper walked out very pale but very determined-looking. He had been put against a wall and the Black and Tan, who was a good shot, fired at him so that the bullet just missed his head.

A night or two later this Black and Tan's closest colleague was courting a girl, who defied the I R A's rule of non-fraternization, when a rifle bullet fired from the dark thudded into the wall beside him. The Black and Tan saw the girl home and returned to the barracks for his rifle—whilst courting he carried only a revolver and a Mills bomb—and went off into the dark on his own to find the spoil-sport.

Fifteen years afterwards I was in Ayr, in Scotland, when this Black and Tan's name—an unusual one—caught my eye on a local advertisement. A friend of mine and myself put on raincoats and trilby hats and called at his house. His mother told us he was still in bed but we told her we were friends and she told us to go on up to his bedroom. We knocked and he bid us enter. We stood at the end of the bed with our right hands in our pockets and asked him if he had been a Black and Tan in Ireland. If he was at all disturbed he did not show it. "I was," he said. I told him how I had remembered him and we shook hands and for the next few days he entertained us royally.

I remembered seeing him one day at the window of the police barracks with a rifle pointed and a crowd of people coming out of Mass. His friend from the North of Ireland was standing in the square taunting the worshippers as they passed. The men luckily did not rise to the occasion—or if they had our friend in the barracks window would have made another martyr for "auld" Ireland.

There was an R I C sergeant in charge of the barracks but the Black and Tans ignored him. On moonlight nights a group of them used to walk up and down the village streets shooting down chimney pots until the village ran out of them. They would pick a house at random and thump at the door with their rifle butts. Every householder was forced to pin up inside the door a list of people sleeping in the house. The Black and Tans would examine this list and might decide to search the house, and if they found anybody not accounted for on the list they would arrest him or her.

Eventually to the relief of the villagers they would return to their fortified barracks, which was a large house fitted with steel shutters. The windows were sand-bagged and barbed wire erected all around. As further protection, land mines were placed at strategic points within an area of 100 yards of the barracks. These mines were placed behind walls, trees and anything that might give cover to the I R A attacking the building. The police also broke holes in the walls of the barracks to within an inch or so of the outer wall. If they were attacked they broke through this mortar skin and dropped bombs through the holes.

These precautions were usually quite useless because the I R A found out where the mines were placed and where the holes in the walls were situated.

Frequently after the Black and Tans had returned to barracks an I R A man fired a couple of shots at the windows. This was sufficient to cause all hell to break out—every policemen took up a position and fired shots in return. The luckless villagers knew then that they were in for a sleepless night and would retire to cellars or under their beds.

The I R A man remained safely out of sight, but if the police firing died down he would fire again before jumping on his bicycle and going home happily for the night. But now the police exploded the land mines, which were fired by electricity through wires from the barracks. Showers of stones and soil rained on the roofs of the houses. The police then sent up distress rockets and fired Very pistols which turned the night into a synthetic day—and all the time their rifles and revolvers and automatic pistols kept up a futile fusillade. The military were stationed thirteen miles away and when they saw the rockets they turned out on their lorries and drove hell-for-leather for our village. Often they stopped to remove trees, which had been felled across the road, or bridge trenches that had been dug in the road, and they would be convincing themselves that the police were fighting off a murderous attack.

Eventually they would arrive at the police barracks to be told that hundreds of armed men had been beaten off. Then the military might decide to search houses in the village and would round up all the men they could find to fill in the road trenches. Usually only old and very young men were used for this, because the able-bodied knew what to expect and vanished when the military came.

Such incidents as this were frequently repeated and kept the police in a very jittery state of mind because they could never guess when the I R A were going to make a serious attempt to capture the barracks. When the I R A decided to capture a barracks they usually succeeded, using dynamite, gelignite and petrol to hasten the operation.

One fine summer's day the Black and Tans of our village went for a swim in the nearby river. They all swam in their pelts, leaving one of their number to watch over the piles of uniforms and arms. The pool where they were swimming was overlooked by a wooded hill. As they were happily splashing about, a few shots rang out, spattering the water. The Black and Tans suffered heavily from the briars into which they dived but nobody was hit by the bullets. One of them streaked for a flock of sheep and hid amongst these animals, scrambling along as the sheep bolted away from him. He managed to keep up with them until they came near a fence, when he too dived through a briar hedge and ran towards the village. Remembering his lack of attire he ran into the first cottage he came to, where he found an ancient lady, who told him that she had no such things as a pair of trousers in the house. She offered him a skirt which he wrapped around himself and padded on to the barracks.

His story of showers of bullets hitting the water and his assurance that he was probably the only survivor really panicked the garrison, who now gave the villages another treat. They fired daylight distress signals. These soared high into the air, exploding with terrific detonations and giving off great clouds of brick-red smoke. The military heard them and came running again to hear another story of attacks by hordes of Sinn Feiners and probably to wonder why there were no casualties.

There was one casualty and that an unfortunate one. Every day the police—R I C and Black and Tans—used to form a patrol of about fourteen men and walk a mile or so into the country and back. Two Black and Tans argued one day about whose turn it was to go. They ignored the sergeant and it seemed as if they were going to fight, so one old decent R I C man said he would go and his offer was accepted.

They had hardly gone 100 yards from the barracks when a machine-gun operated by an I R A man opened fire on them. One man dropped dead riddled by the bullets—and he was the peacemaker.

They did not carry out police duties, so the I R A set up their own police force. This meant that the I R A also set up their own courts and the British courts were boycotted. There was a need for civil police at this period because civil offences took place from time to time. The various taxes which should have been paid to the British were collected by the I R A whenever possible—except dog licences. I remember once seeing the whitewashed walls of the British court-house decorated in huge black letters of tar with the legend, painted by the

I R A: "Dogs paid for will be shot." Thus the policy of the I R A, aimed at making it impossible for the British to rule, was being achieved.

The Black and Tans became a terror force and as such were quite a success. A paper called the *Weekly Summary* circulated amongst them from Dublin Castle, and this organ whipped them up to a frenzy of hatred against the "murder gang", as the I R A were called. They only made contact with the I R A when the I R A chose—and then, sensibly, the I R A, whose job it was to live for Ireland not to die for it, did not give prior notice of their intentions.

"The indisputable source of all crime is the organized gang of assassins which describes itself as the I R Army. This gang of assassins is a peril which must be stamped out at all costs," wrote the *Weekly Summary*, and, "The R I C must put out the murder gang. It is war to the death." [7]

The paper's most outstanding effort was, undoubtedly, the following which was published in October 1920—it was a proclamation issued during the American Civil War by General Price who was Federal Commander of West Kentucky:

"I shall shoot every guerilla and if you shoot one of my soldiers I shall walk out five of your rich bankers, brokers, and cotton men and shoot them. . . . So help me God." The *Weekly Summary* strongly recommended this procedure as an efficient way of restoring law and order.

The R I C-cum-Black-and-Tans organization was leavened throughout by the I R A intelligence organization. There was not a barracks in the country in which at least one of the men was not an I R A agent unknown not only to his companions but to the local I R A. This, indeed, led on a few occasions to Collins's men being shot. One such case happened in Cork City. [8] The Lord Mayor of Cork, Terence MacSweeny, was

National Museum of Ireland

This daylight landing of rifles for the Irish Volunteers at Howth in 1914 led to the first killings of Dublin people by British soldiers. The operation was the work of the Englishman Erskine Childers (right) whose wife, holding a rifle, is seen aboard the *Asgard* with Mary Spring Rice, cousin of the British Ambassador in Washington.

Gael-linn

Michael Collins

Tom Barry, the brilliant guerilla leader who, amongst many exploits, led the I R A force which wiped out the Auxiliaries at Kilmichael.

arrested whilst in possession of an R I C code which could only have come from an official source. Some time afterwards the Cork I R A were ordered by Collins to kidnap a certain R I C sergeant, which they did. Not only did they capture him but in their enthusiasm they executed him—quite wrongly because he was, in fact, the member of the I R A intelligence force who had passed on the code, and Collins's order to kidnap him was meant to save his life. Collins feared that he had been discovered by the British authorities.

The intelligence system founded and organized by Collins had agents everywhere—in Dublin Castle itself as well as in the post offices and in every public service in Ireland, and not only in the Dublin police headquarters but in Scotland Yard in London too—and these agents were helped willingly by the overwhelming majority of Irish people at home and overseas.

The police had ceased to be the eyes and ears of the Government. When they were not confined to barracks, they walked about in heavily armed patrols. Informers were few and any that did give information to the police were reported by the agents in the police itself.

One treacherous member of the I R A in Cork County was tempted by an offer of £500 to tell the police the name of a farm where an officer of the I R A was hiding.[9] Police surrounded the farm-house within a very short time and called upon the I R A officer to come out. Not receiving a reply they rushed the house and outhouses firing as they went but, apart from the farmer's wife, found nobody. The I R A man was in fact looking down on the activity from the shelter of a wooded hill.

Shortly afterwards the leader of the local I R A was told the name of the informer. Instructions were at once issued that this man was not to be allowed to leave the district, and a court-martial was convened at which an officer from Dublin attended. The court decided that the traitor should be executed by shooting at the first available opportunity.

There was a dance a few nights later and the condemned man, unaware that his treachery had been revealed, attended because he had been told that a girl on whom he was very keen had sent a message hoping he would be there. The girl was also told to attend and to dance with him a couple of times, then to arrange to meet him after the dance at a nearby gate, but she was warned to go straight home and not to approach the gate.

Everything went as arranged and the traitor turned up to find four armed men waiting. They tied him to a gate-post, bandaged his eyes and shot him. Before they left they pinned a little card to his coat: "Spies and Informers beware. I R A".

Such incidents as this gave the Black and Tans what they considered to be an excellent idea—they dressed in civilian clothes, put on masks and called on houses in which suspected I R A men lived. In several cases they took the men out, blindfolded and shot them and placed little cards on the bodies, with exactly the same wording. They were ignorant of the I R A agent in their midst. This trick boomeranged.

In July 1920 a new British force appeared on the Irish battlefield. This new force was called the Auxiliary Division of the Royal Irish Constabulary, but in fact it was quite independent. The Black and Tans were paid 10s. a day; the members of this new force were paid £1 a day out of which they had to pay mess fees It was advertised in London as a Corps d'Elite and only men who had held commissions in the British armed services were accepted. The men were interviewed at Scotland Yard in London and if accepted were given first-class single tickets to Ireland and advised to take with them any old

British service uniforms and pieces of equipment they might have in their possession as there was a possibility of police uniforms being scarce.

Each member was given the rank of Police Sergeant but was known as a "Cadet"—and the most extraordinary bunch of cadets they turned out to be. They elected their own officers but took little heed of them subsequently. Their commanding officer was General Crozier who in turn was under General Tudor, and many of the Auxiliaries preferred to be known as "Tudor's Toughs".

They were given no training except in revolver firing and bomb throwing and were posted in various parts of Ireland in commandeered houses. They were a downright nuisance to the I R A, principally because they would not surrender when attacked—preferring to fight it out to the last bullet or the last breath.

This annoying custom of theirs most probably arose because they quite misunderstood the whole Irish question and were utterly convinced that they were fighting a body of callous murderers who would give no quarter. The immediate cause of this was an ambush near Macroom in County Cork.

The force never exceeded 1,500 and in spite of their villainy, their murderings, their floggings and their general marauding, were granted a good measure of respect both by the I R A and the Irish people on account of their undoubted courage under fire. Bill Munro, as nice and gentle a man as you would ever want to meet, joined them in 1920. This is the story he told me, which I have not altered in any way and which is interesting to compare with the account of the Kilmichael ambush given later by Tom Barry, who was in charge of the I R A forces on that occasion.

THE AUXILIARY'S STORY

"In the summer of 1920 London was, like every other city in the United Kingdom, cluttered with unemployed debris from the 1914–18 war, a goodly number of them being officers. Of those ex-officers a majority were in their early twenties, so that subtracting their war service they were mere schoolboys with no knowledge of civilian life, and yet too old to take up boys' jobs. In other words they were unemployable.

"For some months recruiting had been going on for those who became known as the Black and Tans. These were ex-soldiers who joined the R I C as temporary constables and who served with the regular police and had at no time active duty with the Auxiliaries, although some were employed by them as batmen, cooks and so on. Later some of them drove for us.

"To those who are not old enough to remember that year, it will seem incredible, particularly with the full employment after the second war, to learn the means to which some of us had to resort to make a living. There were those who were lucky and could get away to the Colonies but they were few. There were those who addressed envelopes for 5s. a thousand; those who turned hawker to sell matches or boot-laces and such things, in other words became beggars. A number, advertising themselves to be ex-officers, formed themselves into bands of masked street musicians, thus drawing public attention to their plight. There was a public outcry for something to be done and this may have had some influence on the Government. In any case it is a coincidence that about this time it was decided to form the Auxiliary R I C. Personally, however, I never knew of a recruit who came from the hawker or street musician factions, they were not the type who were wanted either by the authorities or by the other recruits.

"Just before this time the representatives of one of the Mexican revolutionary parties had tried to get together a number of ex-officers to go to Mexico to fight for their particular cause. The promises were good—the rank of colonel and a thousand a year—and, despite the advice of the Foreign Office, there were some who were desperate enough to accept the offer. What happened to them is another story.

"It was to men such as these that the formation of a force of Auxiliaries of the R I C came as a godsend. I do not say that all who were attracted to the service were in the same class, there were also older men who were for various reasons without roots. They welcomed it.

"The Corps was advertised as a Corps d'Elite which, of course, made it more attractive, but I doubt if one in a hundred knew anything about the Irish question, as it was then called, nor had they any feelings against the Irish. This was simply pennies from heaven.

"At this late date it is difficult to remember how the news of the new formation was circulated, but it soon got around and many grasped the chance of doing something which was at least remotely similar to that for which the services had trained them.

"The conditions offered were good, particularly for 1920— £1 a day all found, with the rank of Police Sergeant—so it is hardly to be wondered at that the response was brisk, at least at first. We had no idea of what we were to be called upon to undertake. It was a job of work, and although it may appear that we were little more than mercenaries, that was not how it struck us at the time.

"Recruiting offices had been set up in most large towns and thither we went. The main qualifications were service as an officer in any of the three services, physical fitness and the names of references.

"We were not required to wait long before being given tickets to the Curragh, which was then the training centre. Hare Park camp, a disused army hutment, was our depot, the rest of the barracks being then full of the Army.

"We spent about six weeks messing about—what little we got of instruction had very remote relationship to the work we had to do in the country. Theoretically we were put through a shortened police course, having impressed on us the meaning of a misdemeanour and a felony, our powers of arrest, and what we could and could not do. There was a certain amount of arms and bombing practice but all very sketchy, instructors being drawn from our own numbers.

"One incident is, perhaps, worth recording. A party of us were sent to take stock in the clothing stores and, finding a good number of pairs of socks surplus, with the old habits of scrounging, we took a few pairs each for our own use. This in the normal course would have been all right if one of us had not developed a conscience and confessed. The result being that the whole party were taken before Brigadier Crozier and given a very severe reprimand, with the warning of dire consequences in any future episode of this kind.

"The company was composed of four sections, each with an officer ranked as District Inspector 3, in charge, and a Head Constable as his second. These were chosen, not for any experience in the work to come, but mostly by virtue of having held senior rank in the services. In command of the company was a Lieutenant-Colonel rated as District Inspector 1, with a D I 2 as second in command. In the choice of C O, at least, someone was inspired because he turned out to be a wise and considerate officer, who got little credit for the good work he did.

"Towards the end of the training we were issued such R I C uniform as the stores could provide. Naturally the matter of height had not been one of the considerations when we were recruited and as the normal height of the R I C was something over 5 ft. 10 ins. it can be imagined how the shorter recruits fared. By some miracle there was a good supply of R I C caps and we were all issued with one.

"It was not till some months later that we were given the Balmoral-cum-beret that became the only distinguishing mark between ourselves and the R I C constables. The uniforms we got were the usual R I C, that is to say dark green jackets and trousers, and at no time was the official uniform breeches and leggings. Really there were no uniform regulations and we could turn out in a mixture of Army, R A F and Naval uniforms provided we wore the regulation cap.

"Our arms consisted of a ·45 service Webley and a ·303 rifle. Quite naturally, I suppose, some of us were influenced by Western films and wore our revolvers in holsters low slung on the thigh which looked very dashing but which were the cause of quite a number of shot-off toes—as the enthusiasts attempted to emulate the cowboys of Texas. Our stay at the Curragh had been very pleasant, and had included a few nights as guests of the regimental messes. We also attended one race meeting at which our only ex-Scotland Yard member lost his lot on the three-card trick—an incident he never lived down, until he disappeared three months later whilst out trying for information.

"Training came to an end and we were ready to start our job. One day four of us were sent for and told we were the advance party and that our job was to go to a certain town, whose name we would be told at the railway station, and to requisition any building which could accommodate the company and which we thought suitable as a barracks-cum-fort. We were to be in civilian clothes and to be armed with revolvers, much to our chagrin as it turned out.

"At the station we were told to make our way to Macroom, in County Cork, stopping the night in Cork and going on next day. We had first-class tickets and the journey to Cork was uneventful, and although we had been told to be very discreet, we were not too worried, thinking ourselves a very ordinary and unremarkable quartet. On arrival at Cork station we were soon undeceived as the first remark of the jarvey as we got on his sidecar was: 'It will be the barracks, I suppose, gentlemen?' Whether he meant the police or the Victoria Barracks we didn't know, but he seemed rather surprised when we told him to go to the Imperial Hotel. On arriving at the hotel the next remark of the driver shook us still more. 'I suppose it will be the morning train you will be going on,' he said. 'I can pick you up in good time ' On our asking where he thought we were going he said, 'Sure I thought maybe it is Macroom you'd be going to.'

"To say that we were taken aback would be putting it very mildly, we were staggered, but someone had the presence of mind to say we would not want him next day. So much for our look of innocent travellers. Of course the outline of a Webley ·45 in the hip pocket of a light suit is a little noticeable, and our accents were definitely not of the country.

"We booked our rooms and in one of them hurriedly went into conference. We were up against something new, the bush-telegraph here was something we had not reckoned on or indeed understood. If the driver of the sidecar knew who we were and our destination, it was pretty obvious that there were many more in possession of the same information. We were new but we did know some of the implications: four of us in what we had to presume as hostile territory, in spite of being armed or indeed because of it, were a pretty poor insurance risk. Our revolvers began to bother us. It was obvious that we could not go about carrying these massive weapons but it was also exceedingly unsafe to leave them behind, so it was decided that we should take turns to stay and guard them in one of our rooms.

"As I learned years after, we need have had no cause for anxiety as the other side were letting us go in peace for reasons of their own, but it was a bit tricky at the time. Nothing untoward happened and next day Macroom was reached where we thankfully handed over our arms to the local R I C for safe custody. That was the one and only time I ever went armed in civilian clothes, to which I owe the fact that I am still alive.

"After booking rooms at a local hotel the deputation went prospecting for our new home. That was not difficult, there was only one possible building and that was Macroom Castle which was then intact. It was walled on two sides, a river ran on the third side and in front was open domain for a good half mile. So far as situation was concerned the castle was ideal for our purpose and it was decided that we would take over at once.

"The powers of requisition which we had were somewhat vague and on finding that the Castle belonged to a member of the Guinness family we began to have some misgivings as to our success. That the Castle had not been occupied for years and was looked after by a caretaker was somewhat in our favour but we reckoned without the caretaker. This good lady and her daughter were extremely antagonistic from the word go and insisted that without the permission of the Lady owner we would not be allowed inside the place. We found that the owner was not even in the country, had not been for years, and was not likely to come back. We simply walked in and told the caretaker that we were now in possession and that she would in future be confined to her own quarters so far as looking after the premises were concerned, much to her indignation which she was not slow in voicing. She and her daughter were hardly ever seen by us all during our stay.

"The Company were telegraphed that accommodation was ready, and we sat back to await their arrival.

"Three days elapsed before anyone showed up. As they came by road this was not surprising, seeing that some of the drivers were sitting behind the wheel for the first time and barely knew how to change gear. Apparently the journey from the Curragh had been anything but dull although it must have been exasperating to those in charge and not very hopeful for our mobility in future.

"After a short time life became very boring. We were normally on duty every third day and filling in time became a work in itself. Of course we visited the locals but this was rather frowned upon by the Colonel, himself a very temperate man, who did not like too many of us out of reach in case of emergencies. By day we were allowed as much ammunition as we wanted and could go after rabbits and game in the domain, which was a large one. We also did a lot of revolver shooting at bottles thrown in the river. This practice had to stop, however, anywhere near the Castle, as the villagers complained that the ricochets from the water were breaking their windows. The evenings were the worst time and inevitably gambling schools started—any night one could find such games as poker, roulette, crown and anchor, even down to modest nap. These games helped to pass the time and filled the pockets of the bankers, but this too became boring. Naturally, there were no members of the opposite sex as that was taboo on both sides—the local damsels were much more against us than the men. Indeed it was by no means a gay life and we were often glad of an extra night patrol to pass the time.

"Before thinking of doing patrols it was necessary to look into the transport question. Some of the vehicles were in poor shape after their handling from the Curragh and we were sadly lacking in mechanics. Some who had served in mechanized units and others from the Air Force were pressed into service, I being one of the former, and we did our poor best.

"We also had to train drivers and teach them the rudiments, at least, of the working of internal combustion engines, but we were not very successful and there were to be always two or three vehicles off the road until we were lent drivers by the R I C from the ranks of the Temporaries. At this time our transport was made up of ex-R A F Crossley tenders each capable of holding twelve men, and they were very reliable when looked after and driven reasonably.

"To start functioning we had first of all to know what we were supposed to be. It was obvious that we had no real police duties. They were being done by the regular R I C from the local barracks, to what limited extent they could, in the town and the immediate vicinity. We were not the army and in any case there was a company of infantry stationed in the only other large house about the town, so we were starting from scratch on something between the two.

"The C O naturally had some instructions, however vague,

and before long we started patrolling, though with little idea of what to look for. In other words, we were raw.

"Apparently an intelligence officer was necessary to get information about the doings of the other side. There was some difficulty about this as none of us had had any experience of this type of work, but we had in our ranks one who professed to have served with the C I D in London and he was elected. Some of us rather doubted his claim to the C I D as he was the man who had lost his lot on the three-card trick at the Curragh races.

"Whether he ever obtained any real information or not I do not know, but I do know that he sent us careering round Cork and Kerry on many a wild goose chase.

"The usual information was that there was an ambush being prepared at such and such a place, and as a rule it was fairly detailed, giving the numbers and disposition so that we could go to find it in adequate numbers. I hate to think how many of these fake ambushes we hunted. One or two were genuine, I admit, but by the time we arrived they had melted away as they were warned long before we could get near. There were at least two reasons for these timely getaways. The first being their own intelligence, which was excellent, as it should have been, being composed of almost the entire local population. The second reason was that some of our drivers, having become a little enthusiastic, thought they could make their speed a bit higher by making large holes in the silencers of their cars, with the result that our progress could be heard for miles. This practice was soon stopped but it took some time before we could get new silencers from Gormanstown, the transport depot, and I think our friends on the other side must have had many a laugh at us in the interim. On the whole we put in many thousands of miles to no purpose until we became somewhat cagey and wanted some tittle of confirmation of rumours before going tearing off into the blue. This, however, was by no means easy as we had no direct communication with any other unit outside the town.

"Communication was one of our greatest difficulties for the first month or so; then we had naval ratings posted to us with a wireless set and we were able to call up other units within twenty or thirty miles. In theory this was very good but the set was never reliable and the batteries had a habit of running down when they were most needed. Those batteries weighed two tons and we had not the means of recharging them nearer than Cork City. It can be seen therefore that even with wireless, communications were rudimentary. The drill was to take the old batteries into Cork and bring back fresh ones, but even this was not so simple. As I have said earlier our transport was Crossley tenders whose carrying capacity was approximately 15 cwt., which meant that three tenders had to be used to carry the batteries. They could not travel unescorted so at least another three lorries loaded with men had to accompany them, thus losing six cars and thirty men for a whole day during which we were isolated from the outside world, a circumstance of which our opposite numbers made good use.

"Reverting to ambush hunting in general, it became obvious in time that false information was being spread purposely by the other side so that in finding so many mares' nests we would become careless, which, in spite of many warnings by our C O, turned out to be the case and later cost us twenty lives.

"We had been in Macroom for two months and despite all our endeavours we had not been in action or even seen anyone armed or looking aggressive. Really the life was getting a bit dull. To break the monotony, I asked the C O's permission to hire a car for a trip to Killarney. This he gave—not very

happily, it is true, and washing his hands of any harm that
might overtake us. There were four of us in the party, I driving.
I managed to hire a model "T" Ford from the local garage, the
owner of which, I think, was no more happy than the C O.

"I had never driven a Ford so that, looking back on it, the
expedition was foolhardy to say the least. We got away to a
good start, in civilian clothes, and unarmed—that I insisted
on—and had a really pleasant day. Apart from my almost backing the car into a ravine with a river, I managed fairly well.
The next week I was asked by three other friends to repeat the
trip, which I promised to do, but made the mistake of ordering
the car the night before. We started in good style—I was getting used to the Ford by now. Getting near Ballyvourney I was
stopped by a man who strongly advised me to turn back. This
was such an unusual action that I was inclined to take notice,
so I went back to Macroom and told the C O, who at once
ordered four Crossley tenders to scout the Killarney road and
be ready for anything. I joined the party, being acquainted
with the road. We found no ambush but we were taking no
chances and went very slowly. What we did find was a lovely
trench dug across the road just over the brow of a hill, invisible
till one was almost into it. As this trench was about ten feet
wide and the same deep, it would have made a very nice resting place for the old Ford and our four selves. A very easy way
of disposing of four of our number, without so much as a shot.
Quite a few men must have spent a hard night digging that
trench.

"Disappointed of Killarney, we decided the next week to
visit Glengariff. I was unable to get a car from the garage and
so had to commandeer one from a local tradesman who was
not a friendly type. I told him to fill the tank, which he
appeared to do. We got to Glengariff without mishap and

stopped at a hotel just before getting into the town to have lunch and spend a few hours. What caused me to look in the petrol tank I don't know, but I found it almost empty, enough possibly for five or six miles. So our friend the owner had not wanted us to get back. I had the tank filled by a most unfriendly man at the local garage and thought of all I would have to say to the owner back in Macroom. Towards evening we decided to start back, I was not at all keen on doing the journey in the dark. There was a drive leading on to the road from the hotel which was bordered on either side by rhododendrons giving a very good cover. Just before getting to the main road we were startled by a volley of about six shots from both sides of the drive. They were shotguns, we afterwards found, which peppered the old Ford full of dents but, by a miracle, left us unscathed. We all ducked except myself who couldn't because I was at the wheel. My contribution was to make the old car go as it had never gone before and keep it at that. There were no further shots and, apart from what we took to be signal fires on some of the hills along the road, nothing suspicious for perhaps twenty miles. Then, the road turning into a valley, we were confronted by a stationary car facing our direction with its headlamps full on in the middle of the road. There was little time for thought—I was going too fast to have stopped—so I shot over to the left and, not realizing that there was a drop of twenty feet into a stream on that side, took the grass verge with the nearside wheels and just managed to get past. The others swore that the near rear wheel went over into the gully but I was too busy to notice. The occupants of the other car shouted after us but we couldn't hear what they said. To say that we were nervous is an understatement, we were scared stiff. However, we were getting nearer home. There was only one village between us and

Macroom but on approaching it down a hill we saw much more light than was usual and a lot of the lights were moving about. 'Now we're for it,' was what passed through all our minds, but there was no alternative but to keep going, the others ducking on the floorboards. There was certainly some activity in that village. Dozens of men, some with stable lanterns and all of them armed with some sort of firearm, were making their way to the end of the village from which we were coming. Whether it was the fact that they could only see one occupant of the car when they expected four, or whether my time had been so good that we were not yet expected, I still do not know, but we were allowed through with nothing more than a few curses as some of the men jumped out of the way of the car. "Breathing thankfully" is a much worn cliché, but if ever it applied to anyone it applied to us when we were clear of that village. The poor old Ford was beginning to feel the strain and one cylinder was missing badly before we reached home but we made it to the first house of Macroom. Then she finally gave up altogether and despite my coaxing refused to start again. Well, we were home so, leaving the car, we walked to the Castle.

"Needless to say the patrol which, on our information, raided the village found everything peaceful and not a firearm of any kind, and I believe their search was thorough. That was the end of joy-riding for us.

"We had been in Macroom for over two months and during that time peace had reigned in our district. This suited us but it did not suit the other side to have such a large district so law-abiding and seemingly well regulated.

"Our intelligence officer, who, although doing his best had not been helpful at first, was now learning his job and one or two raids on outlying districts had almost brought results, only being thwarted by good look-out men. On several occasions we found traces of very recent meetings, indeed so recent in some cases that we found cigarette-ends still burning. We had not the knowledge of the country off the roads, as had our opponents, and it was impossible to follow up the participants in these meetings. They were able to fade into the country. Usually all this happened after dark and had we gone off the roads there was the danger of being split up and losing our way to be picked off singly. Only in broad daylight and in force was it policy to leave the roads. It was encouraging, however, to find that we were not being led up the garden path all the time.

"Those narrow squeaks must have got the others thinking. One evening our I O went out on an expedition and never returned. We were not unduly perturbed for the first day as he had taken to going farther afield for his information, but after three days we had to conclude that we had seen the last of him and that he was now lying at the bottom of a bog. We never really got to know what his fate was.

"Another I O was appointed but before a week had elapsed he also disappeared. Now we began to be uneasy and to think perhaps our luck was running out.

"Our next I O was sent from H Q in Dublin and was a man of experience who managed to remain alive but got very little information.

"It was during those weeks that we inflicted our first casualty. It was during a raid on some cottages up towards the Kerry border that we apparently surprised a meeting of some sort. It was just some young fellows who took fright on seeing us and ran for it. They were some little way off before we spotted them and they were called on to halt, but they kept going and a few shots were fired after them. They were really out of effective revolver range but by chance one was hit and he fell. On reaching him we found him to be badly wounded so, taking him into one of the cottages, we did what we could for him and sent one car to get a doctor and a priest, both of whom arrived in time to do what they had to do before the young man died.

"This incident depressed us, especially as it was a stupid and unnecessary death and it had, so to speak, opened war, which we had not wanted. The man who fired the fatal shot received several warnings that he was marked and would soon get what was coming to him. So far as I know he is still alive.

"Winter was now coming on and our patrols were no longer looked forward to, indeed they were becoming most unpleasant. We had only open cars and as it rained nearly all the time, as it knows how to in south-west Ireland, we finished each patrol soaked to the skin despite our mackintoshes. This discomfort I think may have been responsible for our disinclination to deviate from known roads. We would take patrols which we knew would only last so long; then we would be back to the dubious comfort of the castle. However it came about, it is certain that each section officer got into the habit of doing the same patrol each time he was on duty. So much so was this the case that, knowing which one was on duty on any particular day, we knew where his patrol was going.

"All this was not lost on the other side. There was always careless talk in the town and it was easy for them to find out which section would be patrolling on any day some days ahead, and make any plans they thought fit. It was in this way that plans were made to ambush No. 2 Section on a certain Sunday.

"No. 2 Section always chose the route Macroom, Dunmanway, Bandon, then back across country to Macroom. The start was usually made in the early afternoon, so there was plenty of daylight left for an ambush to be sprung anywhere before Dunmanway. It was not safe, however, to have it on the main road as there was always the chance of an army patrol coming in the other direction from the troops stationed in Bandon, thus taking the ambushers in the rear. The position was therefore got ready on a side road, which was seldom used, being very rough and having hardly any houses along it, about half a mile away from the main Macroom–Dunmanway road. There was one weak link in their strategy—that was to get the patrol off the main road without raising suspicion. Here they showed their knowledge of the characters of our various officers. The leader of No. 2 Section was not a quick thinker although sound enough; he was also of a very trusting and unsuspicious nature. The patrol was late in getting away as one of its number was absent, curiously enough an Irishman, but having waited some little time it started one man short.

"Some miles short of Dunmanway at the junction of a side road the patrol was stopped by a civilian, who said he had been sent by the officer of an army patrol of two lorries to say that they had broken down and were in need of help a little way up the side road. Now to a quick thinker several things very wrong in this situation would have been apparent. Why was an army patrol on that road at all with its bad surface and unimportance? Why had the officer sent a civilian, who must be supposed untrustworthy, when with two lorry loads of troops he could have sent an N C O and a few men? In any case the army had no prior knowledge of our patrol coming that way. It is difficult to know what went through our section leader's mind but he turned his two tenders into the side road apparently without suspicion.

"Just as the civilian had said, about half a mile up the side road there were two stationary lorries with a number of men in khaki uniforms clustered round them. Our tenders stopped and our men got out to see what the trouble was, some of them leaving their rifles in the tenders. When they were out

on the road, without any warning whatever fire was opened
up on them from every direction including from the supposed
soldiers. Taken completely unawares, those few who survived
the first volley got down on the road and started to return the
fire. There was no hope of cover. All cover was in the hands of
their opponents so it was inevitably a massacre, which should
only have lasted a minute or two, but there was evidence that
at least three took a long time to kill, although to start with
the odds were twenty to one against us. Out of twenty-one
men, twenty lay in the road dead; what happened to the other
one we never found out. There was a rumour that he had managed to crawl away unseen and had tried to ride a horse, which
had been grazing near, back to Macroom for help. What truth
there is in this we don't know because his body was never found.

"That was the famous Macroom ambush.

"That account of the ambush was gathered, needless to say,
from sources on the other side, since we had no witnesses on
our side left capable of telling the story. However, from the
evidence gathered next morning it is a pretty true picture of
what occurred.

"No news of the ambush reached the company that night,
but as the patrol had not returned by midnight it was evident
that something serious had happened. Volunteers were called
to form a search party and two tenders covered every conceiv-
able road that the patrol could reasonably have taken. The
night was a filthy one, with no moon and rain coming down
in torrents making visibility very poor. That is possibly why no
one was seen as the party passed the junction where the patrol
had turned off. It was said that the same ruse was to be tried
on the search party, and that the ambushers actually waited in
position until after daylight. It is very doubtful, however, that
it would have worked a second time.

"Nothing was to be gained by sending out another search party after the first had returned and it was decided to wait for daylight, or some news coming in, as it was just feasible that the patrol had spent the night at some army post.

"I had not been in Macroom on this Sunday, having driven the C O to Dublin for a conference on the Friday. We left Dublin on the Sunday night but owing to the bad weather and a broken rear spring on the old American car I was driving, we did not reach Macroom until about 9 a.m. on Monday. We had only just arrived, when news was brought in by one of the local doctors, who by virtue of their profession were strictly neutral.

"All available transport was got ready and, with two only of the tenders manned, we set out to bring in all that was left of the Sunday patrol. The doctor accompanied us as it was not known whether there were any wounded.

"There was no difficulty in finding the spot in daylight. There were the two wrecked tenders and, scattered over the road, what was left of twenty of the patrol. All of us had taken part in the late war and we were used to the sight of corpses in far greater numbers than this and in all sorts of conditions. What we saw here was something very different and the difference shocked and nauseated us. In war one is shot or blown up into small pieces. That is luck. Here, however, was deliberate mutilation to make certain that there were no survivors. A strange thing, however, was that one of the worst looking cases was still alive. Even the doctor was amazed that it was possible; he gave his opinion that because of the incessant rain the man's wounds had been kept clean and to this he owed his life. It was far less than a fifty-fifty chance that we could get him to hospital alive, but it was done. He was paralysed for the rest of his life, so it might have been more merciful had he gone with the others.

"It was easy to reconstruct what had happened. Those with no empty cartridge cases beside them were obviously hit by the first volley, and, taking this as a criterion, we could envisage in what order they had died and what sort of a show they had put up. Some had been able to reload once or twice, but the number was soon reduced to three who must have put up a tremendous fight as there were literally hundreds of empty cases beside them. They had fought on even after being hit several times. They must have kept the enemy under cover for a comparatively long time, and it took hand grenades thrown from this cover to silence them.

"After the troubles were over I heard a song often sung in Ireland, composed in honour of the heroes of Macroom, but there were only three heroes there and the song was not in their honour. Perhaps even they were not heroes, since, as we all knew, we could expect no quarter and they were only prolonging their exit by a paltry few minutes.

"We loaded what remained on to the spare tenders and slowly took them back to Macroom, to a town almost as shocked as we were ourselves. This had not been a local affair, it had been too big and too well organized for that. A few of the younger locals might have participated but I really believe that the townspeople knew as little of it as we did.

"Twenty men dead to further the cause, but it did the cause infinite harm because of public reaction on hearing the news.

"For us who were directly concerned the shock had been so great—not so much at the loss of twenty friends, but at the manner of it—that we were like men dazed. Not so the army, who although not directly affected, immediately thought of taking reprisals on the local inhabitants. The houses of some known sympathisers were set alight before our C O could stop it. He ordered us to help in putting out the fires. Our C O took the affair very much to heart. Indeed it preyed on his mind so much that in London after the troubles he shot himself.

"After the first shock had passed our immediate reaction was to hunt down as many of the ambushers as we could and exterminate them. This of course was obviously impossible as our C O soon pointed out. He counselled patience and in good time there would be retribution. He was right as he usually was, quite a few were taken carrying arms, filched from our men, the numbers of which had been circulated. But they were not taken by us, as we were shortly relieved by a later formed company, who had not our inhibitions, and we were posted to Dublin.

"Naturally by Tuesday we were besieged by the press who descended on us in droves, but we were so indignant at copy being made out of our disaster that they got little co-operation. At first they were even barred from the town. Of course we got a very bad press, being called louts, hooligans and many worse names. It would have been better, as we later realized, to have given what was a true account, since the first newspaper versions were far from being accurate. For some reason we were never partial to the press and in consequence suffered its displeasure.

"The stay of the Company in Macroom after the ambush was only a matter of a few weeks, during which time we did our best to get hold of any of the participants who might still be in the district. This was a difficult task as potential informers were much too scared to come forward and the raids carried out were based on previous information. All of those proved abortive. The main search was for arms, by finding which we could prove participation in the ambush should they bear our numbers. No one was foolish enough to hide weapons in houses or outhouses and the countryside lent itself to the hiding of such small objects, so the results were mostly negative. Indeed during our whole stay in Macroom the only arms we discovered were ancient weapons, which had been hidden away, possibly before the birth of that generation and unknown to them. Some I could imagine had been used by the 'Wild Geese', so old were they.

"Our orders to leave for Dublin came as an unpleasant surprise, as it seemed to cast doubt on our ability to handle the position. It appeared that the powers that were considered our methods too civilized. How the company which relieved us fared I do not know, but I do know that they very soon hit trouble in the form of an ambush which developed into a pitched battle lasting a considerable time. This occurred on the Ballyvourney road quite near to Macroom, which left the Auxiliaries' lines of communication open. It ended in more or less a draw.

"Arrived in Dublin we were stationed in Portobello Barracks. Here we found a great difference both in our work and in our social life, not all of it for the better. We were no longer an independent outlying unit, but just part of a large organization receiving our orders from Headquarters.

"Most of our work now was routine, consisting of curfew patrols, conveying prisoners from one place of detention to another, with raids thrown in by way of variety.

"Curfew patrols were new to us and were at first somewhat of a diversion. Our catches were very often innocent enough citizens, who had just overstayed a visit or thought they could chance an extra half hour. Our regular haul were the ladies of the town, who had little respect for us or the regulations. They were always obliging in telling us our fortunes, our ancestry, and what they hoped for us both in this world and the next. All

whom we collected we lodged in the Bridewell and there our
interest in them finished.

"Raiding we also found very different from in the country.
We received orders to search such-and-such addresses. These
searches had to be carried out very thoroughly, with no regard
to the niceties, regardless of the time of night or the situation
of the occupants. Everyone must be got out of bed, beds being
favoured hiding places for arms. No notice was taken of age or
sex, or of their night wear or lack of it. All men found had to
give a good account of themselves, backed by proof, or come
along with us to be lodged in the jail until such time as they
could prove themselves to be reliable citizens. This type of raid
was not popular with us. Most of the houses were in the poorer
quarters of Dublin, where cleanliness was not taken to be next
to Godliness. Occasionally on these raids we did find arms or
documents proving some connection with the movement, in
which cases any man found in the house was automatically
suspect and arrested. There were many distressing scenes as
they were taken away and again we were told our 'fortunes' by
the womenfolk. There were also raids on the better class districts where we were treated with civility, and indeed in some
instances with hospitality, being asked to have a drink before
we started our search. This we had to treat with suspicion and
regard as a play for time while perhaps a suspect was on his way
out of a window or over the roof to safety.

"Important raids were few and far between, but on occasion we got orders to raid certain premises where some high-
ups were supposed to be hiding. These were usually carried
out in strength involving more than one company, so that we
were able to investigate houses on either side of the suspected
one. This was liable to cause confusion since no two companies
were well acquainted with each other, and there being, usually,

some of our plain clothes members with us, it was feasible for the suspect to move about amongst us and make his way to safety without our knowing it. There are quite a few tales of this having happened, but whether any of them are true or just part of the apocrypha of the troubles, I do not know. Certain it is, that all these suspects got away in the most uncanny manner. One thing we were seldom able to do was to get on to the roofs before the alarm was given, and the roofs were the usual way of escape. Naturally, people of the importance of Mr de Valera and Michael Collins were well guarded and warned in time to get away, though it was sometimes a very close thing. We have got into a room where a meal had been in progress a few minutes before, and tea still hot in the cups, but no sign of our man.

"Dublin was not free from ambushes and we had to be on our guard whilst going through the streets day and night. The technique was different from the country. The usual method was for a party to wait in side streets in congested areas and to throw grenades into our tenders or open armoured cars as they passed on the main street, making their getaway in the resultant confusion. To counter this we put a kind of cage of wire netting as a roof to the cars, so that the bombs would bounce off. Then the others put hooks on their grenades to catch on the wire . . . and so it went on until the truce.

"Our company was fortunate in not being involved in any of the Dublin ambushes. Our only fatality was one of our men returning to barracks late at night who failed to answer the sentry's challenge, and was shot dead climbing over the wall round the officers' mess.

"Of the truce and subsequent events I know nothing, as by that time I was in West Africa on a job for which I had applied before joining the Auxiliaries."

TUDOR'S TOUGHS

A c t u a l l y thirty-six I R A men under command of Tom Barry, O/C Third Cork Brigade flying column of the I R A, carried out the ambush on the Auxiliaries of "C" Company at Kilmichael, near Macroom. For the week previously these men had trained—most of them had never before been under fire—and they arrived at the ambush spot at 8 a.m. on Sunday morning after a six-hour march. Each man had a rifle and thirty-five rounds of ammunition.

Up to this time, with the exception of the two who were shot on Bloody Sunday morning, no shots had been fired at the Auxiliaries in Ireland. Their reputation, their appearance and their conduct confirmed that they were a very tough body of men; it became essential to smash the myth that they were invincible.

They were attacked[1] on a level stretch of road surrounded by low stone walls, and the fields and bog land about were marked by some outcrops of large rocks, which gave the guerilla force shelter. It was on the road the patrol always travelled between Kilmichael and Gleann. Barry was concerned how to make the lorries of the Auxiliaries slow down, expecting two vehicles, but there might be three or four. At length he decided that they would certainly slow down if they saw a lone figure in uniform standing by the side of the road, and he ordered one of his men to dress up in the uniform of an I R A officer. There were very few of these uniforms in existence and he gambled rightly on the Auxiliaries' never having seen one.

At 4 p.m. the first lorry load of Auxiliaries arrived and did slow down when the driver saw the figure, but the lorry came on slowly towards a wall, behind which I R A were waiting for the signal to go into action. Then a bomb sailed through the air and landed in the driver's seat, killing him and the man beside him. The lorry continued to advance nearer and stopped only a few yards from the stone wall. A dreadful hand to hand fight followed, the Auxiliaries neither asking for nor giving quarter. They were all killed. In the meantime the second lorry had arrived and stopped about thirty yards away.

Some of the Auxiliaries were lying on the roadway firing, others fought from the lorry. Then one of them called out, "We surrender," and a couple of them threw their rifles away. Three I R A stood up on hearing this. The Auxiliaries immediately shot the three of them, killing two instantly. One of the men fatally wounded was sixteen-year-old Pat Deasey.

Barry called out to his men, "Keep firing. Keep firing. Keep on until the Cease Fire." The Cease Fire was given only when all the Auxiliaries were dead or dying. Then Tom Barry ordered his men to fall in. Many of them were on the verge of shock—it was their first engagement and they had never seen men die violently before. He barked at them, pulling them out of their daze, then he drilled them and as the lorries were set ablaze he marched them up and down through the shattered bodies.

They captured eighteen rifles, 1,800 rounds of ammunition and thirty revolvers with ammunition. Subsequently Tom Barry wrote: "No axe was in the possession of the I R A and no corpse was interfered with. This mutilation allegation was a vicious and calumnious lie. Well one may ask where did Lord French get his information. . . . There were no survivors and no spectators of the fight."

The I R A marched off from the ambush carrying their two dead comrades and young Deasey who was dying; one other member of the I R A had received a head wound which was not very serious. They took with them also the captured armaments and a kitbag full of the papers and notebooks taken from the dead Auxiliaries. Eleven miles away they spent the night sleeping in a deserted cottage and remained there until 4 p.m. next day. During that time large bodies of military who were searching the countryside passed within a quarter of a mile of the empty-looking ruin.

Assessing the fighting qualities of the Auxiliaries after the ambush, Tom Barry, an ex-British soldier himself, decided that their rifle fire was much more accurate than that of the I R A who were, in any case, practically untrained in rifle shooting, and that the Auxiliaries did not like close fighting. He decided therefore that in future the I R A would keep close to them in action. "There are no good or bad shots at ten yards' range," he decided.

In 1921 the British Assistant Under-Secretary for Ireland called on him for a written statement, so that the Government could pay compensation to the dead men's dependants. The Under-Secretary explained that the Government had no evidence of how the men had met their deaths, and that the one last surviving Auxiliary had never recovered consciousness.

After the ambush the Auxiliaries in Macroom Castle posted the following notice in Macroom: "Whereas foul murders of servants of the Crown have been carried out by disaffected persons, and whereas such persons immediately before the murders appeared to be peaceful and loyal people, but have produced pistols from their pockets, therefore it is ordered that all male inhabitants of Macroom and all males passing through Macroom shall not appear in public with their hands in their pockets. Any male infringing this order is likely to be shot at sight.

> By Order.
>
> Auxiliary Division, Dec. 1st, 1920."

It was General Tudor, then Inspector-General of the Royal Irish Constabulary, who recommended the recruiting of the Auxiliaries. It was reported in the *Constabulary Gazette* of July 1920 as follows:

"General Tudor has decided to enlist a number of officers with distinguished war records for service in Ireland. These ex-officers are to be posted to the R I C and their duties will consist of training and co-operating with the police in patrol and defence work. The object is to utilize the war experience and military knowledge of these capable officers with a view to frustrating the raiding and ambush tactics of the Sinn Fein murder clubs.

"Recruiting was opened in London a fortnight ago and over 1,000 applicants have been received. They will rank as cadets but will be graded as R I C Sergeants for the purpose of discipline. Pay £1 per day and uniform, Khaki service dress with R I C badges. Employment guaranteed for 12 months.

"Major Fleming said, 'Great enthusiasm is being shown by the Candidates. It will be the most decorated force in the World. We have already more than one V C, D S O s are quite common and a very large number of the men hold the M C, Croix de Guerre and other coveted war medals.' "

The I R A should have been most impressed. This Corps d'Elite won their first battle honours at a little town called Balbriggan near Dublin. One Tuesday evening in September 1920 a District Inspector Burke, of the R I C, and his brother Sergeant Burke, of the same force, took three "cadets" for a motor drive to Balbriggan. They were actually on their way to a depot at Gormanstown, three miles from the town of Balbriggan. At 9 p.m. they called in for a drink at a public house in the town—a Mrs Smith's. As it was after time, Mrs Smith refused to serve them. An argument ensued and some of the local R I C arrived from the barracks, but when they found out the identity of the travellers they retired. At this time the I R A police were carrying out the normal processes of law and order which should have been done by the R I C. Two Sinn Fein police now arrived and asked the travellers to leave. The Burkes and their cadet friends certainly resented this so they drew guns, the I R A policemen fired and Inspector Burke was shot dead and his brother wounded. In the mêlée that followed the Sinn Fein police escaped.

That night police from Gormanstown descended on the town, and wrecked a good part of it. They burned forty houses, including houses owned by de Valera's sister-in-law. They smashed their way into the house of James Lawley and, ignoring the appeals of his wife and the screams of his nine children, dragged him out and killed him; then they broke into John Gibbon's house and did the same to him.

"Even the first-class carriages on the train were crowded with refugees fleeing from Balbriggan to Dublin next day," reported a paper of the time, "even the first-class carriages!" [2]

In County Galway, the cadets took two brothers named Loughane, tied their legs together, tied the other end of the rope to the end of the police lorry and dragged them over the roads until they were dead. Then they threw the two bodies in a lake. [3]

Captain Nicholas Prendergast [4] who lived in Fermoy, Co. Cork, had but recently returned from the British Army. He had been wounded in France and invalided, but had offered to serve again on the Italian front. There he had been seriously wounded and discharged on medical grounds. In Fermoy he worked as a teacher of languages at a college. Most evenings he went for a drink and a chat to the Royal Hotel and he was there one evening when a lorry load of Auxiliaries arrived. They were drunk and thirsty so they continued to drink but did not pay. Four of the Auxiliaries were chatting to Prendergast when a drunken officer of the Royal Engineers entered and said to them, "Beware of that man, he is a traitor." So they pushed him out into the street, crashed his head in with the butts of their revolvers, and threw his body into the river. They went back to another hotel for another drink and there Mrs Prendergast found them and asked them where her husband was. "Try the Blackwater," said one of them and she went to the Blackwater Hotel to look for him. She saw the point of the "joke" when they fished her husband out of the Blackwater river.

The Auxiliaries then broke into a draper's shop owned by a Mr James Dooley, ordered him out of bed and set fire to the house. The fire spread to adjoining houses and many people had to escape through windows. During the fire they took Dooley to the river and threw him in, then they fired at him with their revolvers as he struggled in the water. He managed to swim away in the darkness and escaped.

When the fire brigade arrived the Corps d'Elite brandished their guns at the firemen and cut the hose. Eventually thirty soldiers and an officer arrived from the military barracks and forced the Auxiliaries to retire.

There had been no immediate reason for this outburst of murder and arson. It was just "high spirits"—the wrong way to win friends and influence good opinion.

Some of the "Tudor's Toughs" stopped in Co. Cork when they saw an elderly man, a priest and a young lad trying to

A typical group of the I R A. This picture was taken after the truce with Britain, and two of the men have acquired both rifles and revolvers. During the fighting a man had considered himself lucky to possess a rifle and more than ten rounds of ammunition.

Gael-linn

Some of the men who helped to annihilate the British Intelligence forces in Dublin. Left to right: M. McDonnell, Tom Keogh, Vinnie Byrne, Paddy Daly, Jim Slattery.

start a motor car—but it wasn't to help. They questioned the youth, Timothy Crowley. Then they put him against a wall and shot him. The seventy-three-year-old priest, Canon Magner, objected so they murdered him. The old man, a magistrate, ran into a cottage and hid. Later he went to the R I C barracks and lodged a complaint about which something had to be done. Later a court martial was held on one Auxiliary, who was found guilty but insane.

The Auxiliaries were not all bad by any means. One of them saved the life of David Hogan in a Dublin room. He covered another Auxiliary with a revolver as he was about to shoot Hogan and the pointing gun dissuaded the would-be murderer. David tells the story excellently, as he tells every story, in his book *Four Glorious Years*.

In Cork county an I R A leader, James O'Beirne, once had three prisoners on his hands—a spy and two members of the Auxiliaries. Local chiefs were not allowed to execute suspects without permission from the headquarters of the I R A in Dublin. Within a few days instructions were received to shoot the spy and this was done. Some days later instructions were received to shoot the Auxiliaries. By this time the two Auxiliaries, who had given their parole, had become very friendly with their captors—they helped to cook and wash up, played cards and proved to be a couple of really decent chaps.

When the I R A officer received his orders to shoot them, he first of all withdrew the parole. The two Auxiliaries knew immediately what this meant, and when later that night they were ordered to dress and get ready for a walk, they knew that they were going to be shot. The leader walked them a long distance from the house, so long that one Auxiliary said, "Why make us walk all this way—why not do it here?" O'Beirne told them to keep walking. After a time he told them to stop and said, "Keep on walking now till you come to a lamp-post —turn right there and it will take you to your barracks." "So you are going to shoot us in the back," said one of them bitterly. "Keep on walking," said O'Beirne. And they walked gingerly away. When they found that they were not going to be shot they stopped and one of them came back. "But what will happen to you if you don't shoot us?" he asked. They were not all bad fellows.

As you might expect in a book there is a fairy tale sequel to this story—but it is not a fairy tale. O'Beirne was on duty later in Dublin when he was caught up in one of the sudden street checks Auxiliaries at that time carried out. He was lined against a wall with other men and he had a pistol in his pocket which meant death for him if he was discovered. As an Auxiliary walked down the line frisking the men another Auxiliary came across and said, "Leave this bastard to me." He struck O'Beirne across the face and kicked him along the street until they passed beyond the cordon. Then he gave him one final kick and said: "We're quits." Only then did O'Beirne recognize him as one of the men he had allowed to escape.[5]

In Dublin the newspapers went on producing night after night, and this meant that the staff remained on the premises all night because there was a curfew after 10 p.m. After that hour anybody found on the streets was arrested; several were just shot. There were men, of course, who risked going home about three o'clock in the morning, but it was quite a chance to take.

Sports sub-editor on the *Irish Independent*, an Irish daily paper of the time, was George Gormby.[6] One night the door of his office was opened and two figures wearing raincoats entered. They took off their raincoats and proved to be two tough-looking Auxiliaries. "Excuse me," said one of them politely, "I'm Lou Williams, heavy-weight boxing champion of Australia, and I wonder if you could help to arrange a fight between me and Dave Magill, heavy-weight champion of the R I C?" Williams and his friend who was addressed as "Ginger" sat down and a cordial chat followed. Williams explained that he had come to England seeking fights, but could not get a match. When his money dwindled he joined the Auxiliaries. He was not interested in the Irish nor in fighting them—all he wanted was boxing matches.

Gormby, a member of the I R A, was also a keen boxing man, and with enthusiasm set about fixing up the fight. It had to take place in the R I C depot at Phoenix Park, in Dublin, because if it was held in a public hall the I R A might intervene. Magill beat Williams.

Some weeks after the fight Gormby finished his work on the paper about 2 a.m. and decided to risk the curfew and make his way home through the back streets. He took his shoes off, tied them around his neck and started padding homewards. All went well until suddenly he tumbled over two figures lying on the pavement—they turned out to be an Auxiliary and a lady of the streets. Another Auxiliary was similarly engaged in the roadway.

The two men immediately got to their feet and flashed torches on George, who was now streaking off as fast as his stockinged feet would carry him. He ran around a corner and went slap into another figure—another Auxiliary, who was knocked unconscious by the force of the impact. This Auxiliary's companion caught George by the neck and threw him against the wall. "What the hell is this?" said the Auxiliary, and George recognized Ginger's voice. "It's me, Ginger—George," he said and quickly told him what had happened—and stretched on the ground was the heavy-weight champion of Australia! Between them they brought Lou round and the two Auxiliaries escorted George to his lodgings. On the way George told them how he had lost his shoes in the chase. Next morning the missing shoes were side by side outside the door with the milk. George, who is a slight figure, said, "I must have been terrible nervous to knock out the Champion."

On Patrick Street Bridge in Cork City one afternoon James O'Beirne saw a Black and Tan smoking a cigarette and gazing reflectively at the passing waters of the river Lee. James put an unlit cigarette in his mouth and strolled across to the soldier and asked him for a light. As the policeman held his lighted cigarette to the unlighted one, James stuck a revolver in his stomach and said, "I will have your revolver—and no trouble." If anybody passing noticed what was happening they gave no sign. The Black and Tan handed over his revolver which the I R A man slipped into a pocket. Then the policeman said: "Hit me, I can't go back to the barracks untouched." "It was the most unwilling blow I ever struck in my life, but I hit him hard and made his nose bleed and he went off happily," James told me. They were not all bad fellows.

In addition to 11,000 fully armed R I C and Black and Tans and 1,500 armed Auxiliaries there were 40,000 British soldiers in Ireland and odd groups such as an independent force called "permanent raiders". One well known B B C producer told me that he was a "permanent raider". These raiders were formed from British officers who had returned from fighting with the "White Army" in Russia and could find nothing better to do in any other British trouble zones. The group included an officer named Read, who had won the V C. When they reported to an R I C sergeant at Tullamore, Co. Offaly, the sergeant looked at them and said, "And what jail have you lot of bastards come out of?" In addition to all these there were groups of independent intelligence agents, many of whom were professional assassins, who murdered callously and efficiently and without any slight tinge of remorse or even interest.

The Auxiliaries were sent to those parts of Ireland where I R A activity was greatest, and Michael Collins said that it was a great compliment to the local I R A when the Auxiliaries were sent there. Their presence, however, always meant trouble for the local people—bad trouble.

Brigadier-General Crozier dismissed a number of these men from the force for various crimes,[7] but on 1 November, 1920, his powers of dismissal were taken away from him by higher authority.

The I R A of Cork City and County were a sore trial to the forces of the Crown, and in return the men, women and children of the area suffered badly. In sober truth the British forces were defeated time and again by civilian soldiers, and the military and police—with a few outstanding examples— played hell with the unarmed people.

The heroic sacrifice of the Lord Mayor of Cork, Terence MacSwiney, was one of the greatest of the gestures which recruited world opinion to the cause of the Irish. In *Rebel Cork's Fighting Story*, published by *The Kerryman*, Tralee, Co. Kerry, several of the Cork I R A leaders tell their own accounts of their battles with the British. The following are some of the incidents described.

The Cork I R A captured twelve rifles from the Cameron Highlanders and in return the Scottish soldiers shot an un-armed blacksmith dead.

The I R A captured the military barracks at Mallow, Co. Cork, and shot one courageous sergeant who resisted, and in return hundreds of drunken soldiers burned and looted the town, watching terror-stricken women and children running to the house of their parish priest where they felt safe. There were only women, children, and old people in the town when it was destroyed because every able-bodied man with a grain of sense in his head made himself scarce.

Men of the Essex Regiment shot an unarmed member of the I R A in Kilbrittain, Co. Cork, and were subsequently attacked by a column of the I R A, who killed four of them. The Essex surrendered and handed over their rifles, revolvers and 2,000 rounds of ammunition.

Ten men of the Cork brigade held up the crew of a Naval sloop at Bantry and captured all the arms and ammunition on the ship. The British determined to wipe out the I R A in that area once and for all time. Hundreds of troops deployed, aeroplanes flew overhead and huge areas of the country were encircled and scoured, but the will-o'-the-wisp I R A never turned up in the bag.

At Coolavokig, Co. Cork, sixteen Auxiliaries were killed and eighteen injured, before a long convoy of lorries and armoured cars packed with troops arrived to relieve them. The Auxiliaries fought bravely on that occasion. An I R A sniper reluctantly shot Major Seafield Grant dead as he stood erect under a withering fire. He was trying to establish the position of the rebels as his men, seeking what cover they could, returned the fire.

At Clonbanin, Co. Cork, the rebels waited to challenge a convoy of over twelve lorries and an armoured car, which was escorting Brigadier-General H. B. Cummins, D S O. Before arriving at the ambush the General sent half the convoy back and arrived with three lorries, a motor car and an armoured car. The ambush started as arranged and the I R A called upon the General to surrender. "Surrender to hell. Give them the lead," he replied and dived to the side of the road. A minute afterwards he was shot dead. He was the first officer to adopt the habit of conveying a civilian hostage in the soldiers' lorry—he had one that day but it didn't help. In the general confusion the hostage took to his heels and escaped.

At Crossbarry, Co. Cork, the I R A, led by Tom Barry, defeated a force of 900 military. On this occasion the military were aware that the rebels were in position and they encircled these positions. There was also a hostage in one of the military lorries on this occasion, who escaped to join the rebel forces; while a piper, Florrie Begley, playing Irish war music, was with the rebels throughout the battle. One group of 300 men of the Essex Regiment was under the command of Major, later General, Percival, who was in charge of the British forces at Singapore when it surrendered to the Japanese in World War II.

The Auxiliaries began to use armoured trucks with machine-guns pointing fore and aft, which gave them a decided advantage in their fighting with the I R A. At Rathcoole, Co. Cork, I R A columns—sixty-five with rifles and fifty with shot-guns—attacked four such lorries. The British fought with remarkable courage and determination, even attempting to outflank the I R A. After a battle which lasted an hour the I R A withdrew without casualties. Half the Auxiliary force had been killed and several wounded. The following day, when the I R A were miles away, Auxiliaries and military raided the district, burning down a wood and killing two young men whom they came across.

At Middleton, Co. Cork, a fully armed cycle patrol of twelve men of the Cameron Highlanders and one R I C man were tackled by ten I R A armed with three revolvers. The I R A captured eleven rifles and bicycles. Apart from hurt pride there were no injuries. At a subsequent court martial one of the soldiers swore that he had been held down on the road by ten I R A and surrounded by thirty of them who were all armed with rifles and bayonets.

The night of the ambush the Highlanders made Middleton a most unhappy town with their raiding and pummelling and shooting. The police in the barracks heard the soldiers shooting and thought they were being attacked, so they started shooting as well and several luckless animals were killed.

At Clonmult, Co. Cork, a British ex-serviceman hunting rabbits discovered that a group of I R A were living in a disused farm-house. He sold the information to the military for £30—and this is one of the exceptions which proved the rule about informers in Ireland during that period. A company of the Hampshire regiment surrounded the house. As they approached two of the I R A men were at a well filling a bucket. They ran back to the house and on the way were fatally wounded. The other sixteen men in the building refused to surrender and a fierce battle ensued—during the fight the soldiers were reinforced by Black and Tans. The thatched roof of the farm-house was set on fire and when the position was completely hopeless what was left of the I R A agreed to surrender and walked out unarmed. The first seven were mown down by the Black and Tans. The British officer, running up, stopped the police from killing three others who came out carrying a wounded comrade. The British captured three wounded men and six unwounded. Two of the latter were hanged in Cork jail, the others sentenced to heavy terms of imprisonment. The informer did not live long enough to spend his £30.

Major-General Philip Armstrong Holmes, Divisional Commissioner of the R I C, had replaced Colonel Smyth who had been shot dead in the County Club in Cork. Holmes and a party of R I C were ambushed at Tureengarriffe. Holmes, though fatally wounded, refused to surrender until all the R I C ammunition was exhausted—by then all the policemen had been wounded. When they surrendered they were given first aid by the I R A who commandeered a motor-car to send the Divisional Commissioner and the most seriously wounded to hospital at the County Infirmary.

Next day the Black and Tans arrived in the district and enjoyed their first experience of firing on a football game. In this case it was only children. They killed young Kelliher, aged fourteen, and wounded two nine-year-old boys. Then they bombed and burned homes and shops in the village of Ballydesmond.

But the activities of the I R A in and about Cork City and County and their refusal to be intimidated by superior arms and the campaign of terror could only have one end—some well thought out devastating reprisal. It came with the planned sacking, burning, and looting of the city of Cork itself.[8] On a night when it was defended only by its old men, women and children the gates of the military and Black and Tan barracks were opened and on lorries and on foot the uniformed forces of "law and order" were released for one uproarious night of vandalism. Being traditionalists they went first of all to inns and bars of the city where they drank what they could and destroyed what they could not take with them; then to the jewellers' shops and stores; then with petrol and incendiaries they set the rest ablaze.

Cork is an ancient and beautiful city on the banks of the River Lee, peopled by citizens who differ in some ways from the rest of the Irish people. They are hard-working and generally speaking more at home with business and commerce than the rest of the Irish. In the fighting they took their shrewd and resolute character with them and caused the British forces more trouble than most of the other counties. There is a lot of truth in the song Corkmen sing, which acknowledges the help given by other counties but finishes up: "But the boys who beat the Black and Tans were the boys from the County Cork."

And the burning of Cork was one of the Black and Tans' greatest defeats. That night the Auxiliaries, side by side with the Black and Tans and helped by the military, turned out for their gigantic event. At that time martial law had been declared in that district, so the military were technically in charge, but they made no move to maintain order. Curfew was supposed to begin at 10 p.m., but the enraged police drove people off the streets long before curfew. A wild and drunken mob of police and soldiers ran a mad riot whilst the citizens trembled, wondering when the pogrom would begin. But they killed only two citizens that night—the brothers Delaney, in front of their father and sisters.

Then they set fire to the City Hall and all the buildings in Patrick Street—the main boulevard of the city. When the fire brigade turned out, they cut the hoses. Apart from the loss of life they caused £3,000,000 worth of damage in their frenzied outburst.

And in the House of Commons in London a few days later the Chief Secretary for Ireland blandly explained that the people of Cork had, in fact, set fire to their own city. He further explained that a spark from Patrick Street set fire to the City Hall—nobody had thought to tell him that it was 600 yards away and that a river intervened. One London paper published a fake map of Cork to show how this could have happened, inserting the City Hall a long way from where it is actually built.

"K" Company of the Auxiliaries took the whole matter light-heartedly and did not even try to understand why politicians refused them the credit they deserved. This company of ex-British officers were, in fact, so proud of their achievement that they replaced their cap badges with burnt corks.

As Cork burned that night one disciplined army watched it. Around the city were various groups of the I R A watching the flames and, with great hate in their hearts, the exulting police and soldiers. The Crown forces—the agents of law and order—were playing their paltry parts. "We could have shot most of them that night if we had wanted to," a Cork I R A leader told me, "and we wanted to all right, but it would have ruined the whole show. They were doing all they could to help us."

The overall military commander was Sir Henry Wilson, who was Chief of the Imperial General Staff. He was a rabid enemy of the I R A, he did not understand them, and he had no patience with any Irishmen who talked about independence—once advocating the shooting of I R A members and their sympathizers by roster. He was strongly in favour of the Government putting a system of official reprisals into effect. Reprisals were, of course, semi-official, but as he said in his *Diaries*, "If the Irish are going to be murdered why shouldn't the Government murder them?" The local commander in Ireland was General Sir Nevil Macready, who had previously been Commissioner of the London Police.

Macready was one of the few who clearly understood the policy of the I R A leaders. He knew that what the I R A wanted most of all was undisciplined and barbaric activity by the British forces. The Black and Tans and Auxiliaries and

Intelligence murder squads were providing the material that Collins wanted and Macready did all he could to make his soldiers behave themselves. It was due to his endeavours that —with a few exceptions—the British Regular Army in Ireland maintained a good reputation. It consisted mostly of young soldiers, as the battle-trained ones had been demobilized after the end of the 1914-18 War.

Soldiers got out of hand in Fermoy after one of their colleagues had been killed by the I R A in a raid for arms. They killed one civilian and burned and looted the houses of men who had served on a jury at the inquest on the dead soldier. The jury had returned a verdict that he had died "from a bullet wound caused by some person unknown"—which was true enough. But the soldiers wanted a verdict of murder against the I R A.

In June 1920 General Lucas, Colonel Danford of the Royal Artillery, and Colonel Tyrell of the Royal Engineers were fishing for salmon on the river Blackwater. Liam Lynch, who was in charge of the Cork No. 2 Brigade of the I R A, and three of his officers captured them. Lynch and one of the I R A, Paddy Clancy, ordered the General and Colonel Danford into a motor-car, got in with them and drove away.

On the way the two British officers spoke to each other in Arabic and then, suddenly, threw themselves at their armed captors. The car ran into a ditch and a fierce fight followed between the four men. Lynch eventually subdued Lucas but the English Colonel was throttling the life out of Clancy. Lynch, now with his revolver in his hand, ordered the Colonel to surrender, but he ignored the order so Lynch shot him in the jaw. The other car with the other Colonel and the I R A now reached the scene of the fight and the I R A decided to leave the unwounded Colonel Tyrell to look after

Colonel Danford. They drove off with General Lucas, who was kept in captivity for a month. During captivity he was treated with every respect and in discussing the "troubles" gave it as his opinion that "the I R A were going the right way about it this time". Interviewed by the Press afterwards about his captivity he said, "I was treated as a gentleman by gentlemen."

But when the British soldiers at Fermoy heard about the capture of their General and the shooting of the Colonel they ran amok and once more the old men, women and children of Fermoy experienced the blind wrath of undisciplined British soldiery.

At Templemore, men of the Northamptonshire Regiment smashed the town up, some of them putting on ladies' dresses, which they had looted, to amuse their companions.[9]

In Bandon, officers of the Essex Regiment tortured two men named Hales and Hart.[10] After beating them up they strapped the two men together and placed a charge of gun-cotton between them. The officers had no detonator with them so they did not proceed with killing them—if, indeed, they ever had that intention. They took the men to Bandon military barracks and after further beating placed them in front of a firing squad. Hart was barely conscious—the officers stuck a little Union Jack in his hand. They changed their minds again, dismissed the firing squad and went to work on Hales with pincers. Hart went out of his mind and was sent to a lunatic asylum. Hales was sent to prison. After this incident soldiers of the Essex Regiment endured a most harassing and unhealthy life.

British soldiers also went berserk at Queenstown (now Cobh), Mallow and Ennistymon, breaking windows, looting and spreading terror and destruction. At Mallow the 17th

Lancers distinguished themselves and were known subsequently as the "Mallow Murderers". At Arklow they lost their patience when taunted by a crowd and attacked, killing one man and wounding another.

Sir Nevil Macready did what he could to prevent his soldiers taking unofficial reprisal action. In August 1920 he urged the Dublin Castle authorities to provide the Auxiliaries with a uniform, which could not be mistaken for that of a soldier's uniform, and the famous Auxiliaries Tam o' Shanter came into being. He was not very concerned with what the Auxiliaries or Black and Tans did, but he did not want the Army blamed.

One of his Orders of the Day dated 22 February read: ". . . three unarmed soldiers of the Oxf. and Bucks L.I. were captured and shot in cold blood at Woodford, Co. Galway. On Feb. 23rd unarmed soldiers of the Essex Regiment were kidnapped at Bandon and murdered.

"Quite apart from the savagery which has always been a marked feature of the tactics employed by the rebels there is no doubt but that these crimes are a deliberate attempt to exasperate the troops, and tempt them to break the bonds of discipline, thereby providing copy for that scurrilous campaign of propaganda on which the rebel leaders so much rely for sympathy in Great Britain and abroad. The Commander-in-Chief looks to the troops, even in the face of provocation such as would not be indulged in by the wildest savages of Central Africa, to maintain the discipline for which the British Army is, and always has been, so justly renowned. . . ."

In September 1920 he wrote to the Chief Secretary for Ireland, who spent all his time in London, expressing his fear that he could not keep the soldiers within bounds. He wrote: "The Army may, generally speaking, be said to be free from any great taint of retaliation and I will take measures to see that every possible restraint is applied. But if the attack on Sir E. P. Strickland [who was in charge of troops at Cork] had resulted in his death I believe that the troops in Cork could not have been held, and that they would have wrecked the town and probably killed many people. This would not have been an ordinary act of indiscipline but the result of an impulse to avenge the murder of their General, under circumstances, when they are aware, that it is unlikely the assassins would be brought to justice by ordinary means. . . ."

He advocated, in that letter, that martial law should be declared throughout the country, so that the police would be subordinate to the military and thus brought under a real discipline.

Luckily for the I R A, the politicians in London turned down the suggestion for general martial law—which was the one measure which could have defeated the whole policy of Sinn Fein.

Sir Nevil in his book *Annals of an Active Life* complains bitterly against the politicians and particularly against the failure of the Government to dominate Sinn Fein propaganda. He urged members of the cabinet to cross to Ireland in order to obtain first-hand information of the state of the country. At a time when every member of the Crown forces took his life in his hands when he left barracks, one M P in the House of Commons asked why troops did not carry their bayonets with them as a protection when out walking!

However, the military eventually did fall in with the I R A's plan, and in September 1920 Macready sent the following notice to every Sinn Fein club in the country:

"In some districts loyalists and members of His Majesty's Forces have received notices, threatening the destruction of their houses in certain eventualities.

"Under these circumstances it has been decided that for every loyalist's house destroyed the house of a Republican leader will be similarly dealt with.

"It is naturally to be hoped that the necessity for such reprisals will not arise, and, therefore, this warning of the punishment which will follow any destruction of loyalists' houses is being widely circulated."

At Middleton in Co. Cork the military subsequently issued the following order:

"As a result of the ambush and attack on police in Middleton and Glebe house, it was decided by the Military Governor that certain houses in the vicinity of the outrages were to be destroyed, as the inhabitants were bound to have known of the ambush and attack and that they neglected to give information, either to the military or the police authorities.

"The houses of the following were duly destroyed between 3 p.m. and 6 p.m.:

Mr John O'Shea; Mr Paul MacCarthy; Mr Edward Carey; Mr Cotter; Mr Donovan; Mr McDorgan; Mr Ahearn:

"Previous to the burnings, notice was served on the persons affected giving them one hour to clear out valuables but not furniture. No foodstuffs, corn or hay were destroyed."

Unofficial reprisals went on alongside the official ones—was there ever such an example of senseless action by a British Government! The people whose houses were destroyed had not the slightest influence on the policy of the I R A. The Government of the Irish Republic congratulated themselves and went on with the policy of infuriating the British forces.

From January 1919 to October 1919 the I R A killed 109 police and wounded 174; killed 16 soldiers and wounded 61; burned 484 police barracks and made 2,861 raids for arms.

THE MURDER GANGS

E v e r y t h i n g was going well with the I R A through the early months of 1920. The Crown forces were reacting magnificently and throughout the length and breadth of Ireland death and terror stalked. The I R A were ambushing, attacking barracks, shooting spies and intelligence men and disappearing into the crowds or into the hills. A few hours later the Crown forces would arrive in strength and shoot, burn and loot. It had dawned on them at last that all the Irish were against them, so they did not trouble to differentiate— to be Irish was guilt enough.

And later the Press of the world would tell the story, the true story of how innocent people had suffered because of the activities of the I R A, and all about the murder gangs, the murder clubs and the assassins. Even the papers which sympathized with the Irish people condemned the I R A "atrocities". However, they distinguished between the I R A and the non-combatants in Ireland, and so consequently condemned atrocities of the Crown forces more vehemently. Everything was going to plan.

But now a new danger to the plans of the I R A arose. The British began to re-organize their intelligence services. Not cleverly, not efficiently, not logically, but sporadically, by guess, and by chance—in the one way, as it so happened, which might be successful.

The I R A could meet a carefully planned intelligence

system, but could not anticipate the haphazard activities of an unreasonable force, nor make provisions for the actions of men ignorant of what, whom, and where they were fighting. Suddenly, unexpectedly and without rhyme or reason, the newly recruited intelligence forces of Britain might swoop and in their ignorant blundering wreck the work of years. The new forces were the most dangerous yet.

It was clear to Collins that success in the fight could only be assured if and when the British intelligence system was rendered useless. Systematically the power of the R I C was undermined. They were forced into armed fortresses and ostracized by the public. Spies and informers were ruthlessly shot. An old lady of seventy, Mrs Lindsay, informed the military that she had seen men of the I R A preparing an ambush. She was kidnapped and shot after the I R A tried to bargain her life for the lives of five I R A under sentence of death. The British commander refused the offer.

Little went on in Dublin Castle or in London that Collins did not know about, but there was no overall headquarters of British intelligence. All the British forces attempted to run their own, and did not pool their information. In Dublin the "G" Division of Dublin police continued to be effective for some months but when, one by one, the more efficient of these were shot down, the rest relaxed their activities. One of the leaders of the "G" Division was an I R A man.[1] His commanding officer called him one day and said, "There is an I R A spy amongst us—I am convinced of it."

"Well," said the spy, "it can only be you or I or one of fifteen others—what shall we do about it?"

"I have just had information," answered the Chief, "that the I R A leaders are meeting at a house in Merrion Square at twelve o'clock today. Now only you and I know, and only you and I will go and arrest them."

The spy knew that his Chief's information was correct, and that Collins, Cathal Brugha and many of the other leaders would be at the house mentioned.

The Chief told him to change his clothes and get his pistol and he remained with him as he did so. Then having arranged for reinforcements to be at hand the two men left the Castle.

As they walked through the street a shot rang out and the Chief dropped dead. His companion lay on the ground and "returned" the fire until his ammunition was gone, then he took the revolver from the dead body beside him and continued to fire that. Troops arrived on the scene, the body was removed and the spy returned to his duties. He said afterwards, "I was sorry I could not tell the Chief who the spy was before I had to shoot him."

Early in 1920 a professional soldier of the Blimp empire-building school was appointed Director of Intelligence for the Crown forces. He was Sir Ormonde Winter, a martinet, who was not prepared to stand any nonsense from the "damned shinners", nor, for that matter, from any of the "damned Irish". He had had experience of intelligence work in India, and he quickly set about installing what he considered to be the normal measures and procedure. He classified the normal channels as: agents obtained by the local police; agents recruited in England and sent to Ireland; persons giving information when under arrest with a view to escape punishment; "moutons" placed in cells with rebels; interrogation of prisoners; listening sets; censorship of letters of prisoners in gaol; Scotland Yard's C I D for information about activities in England and elsewhere; captured documents; the Dublin District special military intelligence branch.

Naïvely he explained afterwards that the only channel that was at all successful was the "captured document" one.[2] His censorship of letters from prisoners proved to be a blessing for many of the grass-widows whose husbands were in gaol. A prisoner would make a reference to the "goods buried in the garden" in some part of his letter to his wife. Subsequently, a lorry load of soldiers would arrive at the house and dig up the garden, never finding anything buried but helping a great deal from the agricultural point of view. Colonel Winter also explained that listening sets in cells proved useless because the Irish accents did not suit them!

He utterly underestimated and misunderstood the Irish and was in fact a typical example of the class that had misunderstood and mis-ruled the Irish for centuries. He imported fifty bloodhounds to catch the rebels, but the rebels, he complained, were unsporting enough to splash disinfectants on their boots, which had the effect of making the bloodhounds sneeze and lose interest in the chase. He was not particular about the methods used to try to extract information from prisoners and was most amused when a rebel who was alleged to have tried to escape from a police tender was shot—by a coincidence, he said, on the same spot where a policeman had died previously!

Winter's squads started work in the Dublin area every night at 11 p.m., and their hit-and-miss raids brought a few successes. From October 1920 to July 1921, they carried out over 6,311 raids and captured a good amount of paper. The Colonel found, however, that a number of his subordinates were retaining certain documents as personal souvenirs and, indeed, that it was not documents alone that his men found attractive.

He was not above using the worst type of criminals for his

nefarious work. One man was charged, he says, with a "heinous" offence. He offered to let him off the charge if he would infiltrate the ranks of the I R A. He arranged for this man to simulate an escape from a police lorry—even arranging a fake ambush—and the man had a measure of success in persuading the I R A that he had genuinely escaped, and was sent to London. Winter provided him with secret ink and a living allowance.

A few days afterwards the body was found riddled with bullets on Staines golf course near London.[3]

All through the war an I R A publication called the *Irish Bulletin* was printed in Dublin and circulated to the press of the world. This paper published authentic lists of British crimes and the background of several of the British personnel. Early in 1920, for instance, when Sir Hamar Greenwood stated in the House of Commons that all the British police in Irleand were carefully chosen and men of integrity, the *Irish Bulletin* gave the following list.[4]

"D. A. Richards of the Auxiliary Division sentenced on Sept. 26th for deserting his wife and children; W. Charman of the R I C arrested for felony Sept. 28th; Alfred Flint, Black and Tan, dismissed on Sept. 29th for stealing a comrade's trousers; Ernest Smith, Black and Tan, died from effects of cocaine poisoning Oct. 4th; Joseph Barclay, Black and Tan, certified a dangerous lunatic, Oct. 4th; Thomas Landers, convicted of thefts in a hotel, asked to be let off with a fine as he wished to join the Black and Tans. Request granted; Laurie Dashington, Black and Tan, caught Nov. 5th stealing a pair of boots in the Angel Hotel, Liverpool. He fired on the person who caught him, and then committed suicide." It also published a secret report from Dublin Castle showing that the Black and Tans at Gormanstown had organized one of the largest ever series of frauds on the British Savings Bank.

By chance, Winter's squad stumbled upon the offices of the *Irish Bulletin* in Molesworth Street, Dublin.[5] They captured all the notepaper, the names and addresses of the recipients, and the typewriter and duplicating machine. Then they had a "brilliant idea".

They made up their own "Irish Bulletin" and sent the forged copies to hundreds of international journalists, M Ps, and United States Senators and Congressmen, whose addresses they now knew.

The forgery was excellent. The contents were not too different in order to maintain its appearance of authenticity. A word or a sentence was interpolated; for instance, "Where true statements [about British terrorism] can be secured this should be done; but, if because of enemy aggression, it is impossible for members of the Dail to visit their constituencies, suitable statements can be prepared from any other source at their disposal."

The *Irish Bulletin* was jealous of its reputation for accuracy and paragraphs such as this could wreck its reputation. The fake edition lasted about a month but the "brilliant idea" never came off at all because Winter missed a day of publication. The same night as he raided the offices, the paper was produced as usual in another place, and its headline was: "The raid on *Irish Bulletin*." The recipients therefore got two copies, but one of them had a wrong number and it was easy for them to spot the fake.

Dublin, being the headquarters both of the British and the I R A, developed into a bloody battle ground. During the day the I R A kept up the pressure by attacking patrols, raiding post offices and shooting key men in the British intelligence services; after dark the midnight murder squads of the British went out in the comparative safety of curfew to raid and shoot at will.

When Colonel Smyth had been shot in the County Club at Cork, after he had urged the R I C to adopt terror methods against the populace, his brother, Major Smyth, then an officer in Egypt, asked to be transferred to Dublin so that he might avenge his brother's death. Colonel Winter appointed him to his intelligence service and he was one of the most active of the midnight marauders. One night with a body of military he surrounded the house of Professor Carolan in Dublin.

A denizen of the Dublin slums called "Bow-tie", who was living on blood-money he obtained from the British, had betrayed the presence of two of the I R A, Sean Tracey and Dan Breen—two of the most sought-after, two of the most dangerous.

Smyth crashed the front door. Breen and Tracey dashed from their beds, seizing their pistols. Smyth and another officer fired through their bedroom door. Breen and Tracey fired back, then dashed on to the landing and emptied their guns at soldiers running up the stairs. Rifles and revolvers were now exploding all round and bullets flying everywhere. The two men, Breen with several bullet wounds, then jumped from the bedroom window and, still firing, made their way through the cordon of military.

Back in the house Smyth lay dead. The senior surviving officer of the British then placed Professor Carolan with his face to the wall outside the room where Tracey and Breen had slept, and shot him through the back of the head. He died next day after he had told the story of the attack.

The brothers Fleming, found in a nearby house, were taken back to the Castle for questioning by Winter's men. Michael was well treated, offered wine and cigars and urged not to be foolish about answering questions. He was told that if he gave information leading to the arrest of the two men who had escaped £10,000 would be paid into any bank he liked to name and that he would be guaranteed a safe passage to any part of the United Kingdom. When he refused he was court-martialled and sentenced to three years' penal servitude —eventually reduced to nine months.

His brother James was taken to Mountjoy Jail and interrogated by Mr McLean, Chief Intelligence Officer, who offered him Egyptian cigarettes and much good advice, and released him. Mr McLean had not long to live then.

And Bow-tie? Some years afterwards, when the troubles had died down, three ex-members of the I R A and a very sick lady were travelling in a motor-car when it came in collision with a lorry. The lorry driver jumped out and one of the men shouted, "It's bloody Bow-tie. Give me a gun quick." The man received a few cuts and bruises as he fought desperately for his life and then broke away across the fields. No one saw him double back and creep up the stairs of a public house outside which the crash had happened.

The lady had fainted and was taken upstairs and put on a bed whilst the chase was going on. As she lay there the door opened and Bow-tie—cut, bruised and terror-stricken—stole in. "In God's name save me—they are going to murder me!" he said. The lady was Miss Fleming, sister of the Fleming brothers and friend of Professor Carolan. She knew Bow-tie well.

They both heard the pursuers calling out and beginning to search the house—and now they were coming to the bedroom door. She pointed to a table covered with a cloth which reached the floor. Bow-tie crept under the table and hid there while the men entered and told Miss Fleming about his escape. When the men left he crept away.[6]

Sometimes in Dublin the arrival of the intelligence squads was heralded by the sounds of motor-lorries and armoured cars being driven fast and coming to a sharp halt. Men would jump from their vehicles, slamming doors and calling out orders, depending upon speed to trap their enemies. Sometimes the squads would move silently, on rubber shoes, surrounding their quarry. Suddenly breaking down a door, they would rush into the rooms, flashing torches and threatening with their pistols anybody they found.

In October 1920, fifty-eight-year-old Peter Carrol whose family was connected with the I R A was awakened one night by the silent squad.[7] They shot him dead, but nobody heard the shooting—they had begun to use silencers.

Two of the most notorious of the intelligence officers were Captains King and Hardy, who added some devilish tortures to interrogation sessions. They beat up Christopher Carberry and made him drink his own blood.[8] Questioning "Bernard Stewart", they beat him practically unconscious.[9] When he refused to speak King heated a poker red-hot, threatened to brand him and scorched his eyelashes. He held a revolver to "Stewart's" head and slowly pulled the trigger . . . the hammer fell on an empty chamber. His victim's real name was Ernie O'Malley, one of the most wanted of the I R A leaders. They did not discover his identity.

The British forces—secret service as well as the rest—tried hard to get Collins, who continued to walk openly through the streets of Dublin without any disguise. Once in the Gresham Hotel, Michael was having dinner with three other members of his organization, when a party of Auxiliaries entered with drawn revolvers. The officer in charge had a

picture of Collins in his hand, the only one they had of him
and luckily a very poor one. He stopped and looked closely at
Michael. He ran his hand through Collins's hair, gazed again
at the picture and moved on. Later that night, according
to one of Collins's closest friends,[10] was the only time
during the troubles that he saw him take a little too much
drink.

In a public house in Dublin on another occasion an Auxiliary
spoke to Collins and asked him to have a drink. They discussed the weather and a few other everyday matters and the
barman put up a pint of stout for Collins. Collins did not
like stout so the barman judiciously poured a little away at
intervals when the Auxiliary was not looking, until the glass
was emptied. Then Collins walked out.

It would have been a dangerous task to try to take Collins
in broad daylight. Twelve of the best shots and the coolest
heads in the organization acted as his bodyguard—they were
known as the "Twelve Apostles". On one occasion two
Auxiliaries stopped him in the street and proposed to take him
for examination—they were not sure but they were rightly
suspicious. Collins quietly advised them to look around, which
they did, to see four disinterested-looking men eyeing them
coldly and dispassionately. The two Auxiliaries walked off.
At that time the Auxiliaries were running a sweepstake
amongst themselves, the amount to be paid to the man who
eventually succeeded in arresting Collins. He had a few other
brushes with the Crown forces in Dublin, on one occasion
getting away by pretending to have had one-over-the-eight,
and on another occasion pretending to be escorting a deaf
and dumb man—one of the twelve apostles.

One agent very nearly succeeded, a man named Jameson,
who began his search by worming himself into the confidence

of the London I R A. His story was that he could help the I R A purchase arms overseas. He came to Dublin with introductions and saw Collins on a few occasions. As there was still some doubt about Jameson, a test was devised: he was told casually that a document he was anxious to obtain was in a house in Iona Drive, Dublin. The house mentioned was, in fact, occupied by a very pro-British family. Shortly afterwards this house was raided by the military intelligence. Jameson was told this innocently, as if it was one of the normal raids, and given another appointment. He kept it—but this time it was his executioners he met.

Another agent named Quinlisk met a similar fate. After meeting Collins and posing as a double agent, he was given an address in Cork where Collins would be at a certain date. A coded message was sent by the British in Dublin to the police in Cork where it was de-coded by Collins's man in the police there. Quinlisk went to Cork on the date and he too met his executioners.

Another agent named Hardy got away with his life, but felt a little foolish about it all.[11] He approached Arthur Griffiths saying that he had a plan to capture the heads of the British Army in Ireland, and was anxious to explain the details of the plan to Michael Collins. Griffiths led him to a room which was full of fierce-looking men and introduced him to the most cut-throat of them all—"Michael Collins". Hardy explained his plans and then Griffiths took some papers from his brief-case and read them out—they were accurate copies of Hardy's correspondence with the British authorities, which had been obtained by the Collins intelligence organization. The men in the room were all newspaper reporters and "Michael Collins" the representative of a Paris daily.

The activities of the British murder gangs ranged throughout Ireland. Old men and cripples were shot, pregnant women, fugitive civilians and children—the murders went on day and night.

John O'Hanlon, at Turloughmore, Co. Galway, was shot in front of his parents, his wife and two small children. At his funeral, Black and Tans came and fired into the funeral procession, wounding several. On their way back to their headquarters in Tuam, they fired at the animals in the field—just for practice. Father James O'Callaghan was shot dead in Cork, and also in Cork city, on the night of November 19th, three men knocked at the door of James Coleman's home. His wife watched him open the door, saw the flashes and heard the explosions of revolvers before her murdered husband dropped mortally wounded.

The men went to the home of Stephen Coleman, no relation of James. Two of them went upstairs to his bedroom and, as he lay in bed, shot him to death to the sound of his wife's screams.

One of the men went to the next landing and into the room of a young man named Hanley, who said, "Don't shoot—I am an orphan and my mother's sole support." Unusual last words and quite futile ones. "Very well," said the assassin as he killed him.[12]

In Galway, a young priest named Father Griffin disappeared one night. A week later his body was found in a hole in the mountainside. He had been shot through the head—a fate which a local schoolmaster had suffered a short time previously.

The London papers were publishing all the details of these murders, the Secretary for Ireland was assuring the House of Commons that these murders were being carried out by the I R A murder gangs, and Lady Londonderry was writing to the papers asking the public to send her articles for the R I C Comforts Fund which she had started.

The Times published her letter in full.[13]

"Dear Sir, I should be very grateful if you would permit me through the medium of your columns to bring to the notice of the Public the great need which exists in the Royal Irish Constabulary in various parts of Ireland where English, Scots, Welsh and Irishmen are serving in that splendid force for such gifts as gramophones, games, books, magazines, writing material and musical instruments—in fact anything that will relieve the monotony of the long winter evenings when these men get their hard earned rest."

Most of them had already found a way of relieving the monotony. In Cork they formed what they called the Anti-Sinn Fein Society[14], and published this decision: "If one of the Crown forces is shot two members of Sinn Fein will be shot and if they cannot be found three sympathisers, including laity and clergy. If a member of the Crown forces is wounded two Sinn Feiners will be killed or two sympathisers." It was better fun than "snakes and ladders".

Five men with drawn revolvers entered the public house owned by Michael Walsh in Galway.[15] He was a Sinn Fein member of the Galway council. They cleared customers out of the house and helped themselves to the money in the till and to free drinks. "We are English secret service men and we know what we are doing," they told his terrified daughter. When they left they took Mr Walsh with them. A week later he was fished out of the river—shot through the head.

Four men called at the Ryans' house in Curraghduff, North Tipperary, and said to eighteen-year-old Margaret Ryan, "We are secret service men over from England."[16] She told them her brother Michael was in bed with pneumonia. They took a candle and went into the bedroom, and there, whilst one of them held the candle, the other fired several shots into Michael—killing him instantly.

Then they moved on to the house of Gleeson (no relation of the author's) at Moher.[17] "Where is your son Jim?" they asked Mr Gleeson. "I have no son named Jim," said Gleeson. "Take him outside and shoot him," said the leader. Fifteen-year-old Willie Gleeson said, "Don't shoot my father, shoot me." "O.K.," said the officer, so they took young Willie out and shot him. His mother and sisters ran out to weep over his shattered bloody body as it lay in the limestone road.

One of the Dublin Castle murder gang—a notorious homosexual and ex-Guards officer named George Nathan—went with a friend to Limerick, and shot the Lord Mayor, George Clancy, dead when he opened the door.[18] Nathan moved on to the house of George O'Callaghan, ex-Lord Mayor of the city, and shot him dead also. Next morning, very boozed and green about the gills, he turned up at the Auxiliary mess in Killaloe and told the Auxiliaries what he had done. It seems they were rather shocked; but then, he was acting under orders.

In Cork city Thomas McCurtain had succeeded Terence MacSweeny, after his death from hunger strike. One night four men with blackened faces called and shot McCurtain dead. The Cork coroner's jury returned a verdict of wilful murder against Lloyd George, the British Prime Minister, members of the British Government in Ireland and District Inspector Swanzy of the R I C. Swanzy was shortly afterwards transferred to a safe district in the North of Ireland, where one day he met three well-dressed men.[19] They drew revolvers and each fired one shot and, as Swanzy lay on the ground they each fired one more shot at him. A Captain Woods, who was near, attempted to interfere, but one of the men fired a shot which shattered the captain's walking-stick and he retired. The three men entered a motor-car and drove away.

This campaign of murder went on all over Ireland. Sometimes the men who were shot had some connection with the I R A, but more often they were innocent. It was a senseless and callous campaign and provided excellent material for Erskine Childers, the English-born Director of Sinn Fein Propaganda.

Sir Henry Wilson, referring to these murders in his diary, wrote: "Lloyd George is under the ridiculous belief, that for every one of our people murdered two Sinn Feiners were murdered, and he was gloating over this and hugging it to his heart as a remedy for the present disgraceful state of Ireland." That was on July 1st, 1920. On September 1st of the same year he wrote: "I told Lloyd George that the Authorities were gravely miscalculating the situation but he reverted to his amazing theory that someone was murdering two Sinn Feiners to every loyalist the Sinn Feiners were murdering. I told him that this was not so, but he seemed to be satisfied that a counter murder association was the best answer to Sinn Fein murders."

With the backing of the British Prime Minister the murders went on, mainly by the murder squads and the Auxiliaries but also by the Black and Tans and, sometimes, the military. To facilitate matters, coroner's inquests were abolished in favour of military inquiries.

In Dublin a random shot from a military lorry killed eight-year-old Annie O'Neill. An inquiry was held by three military officers, but the mother was not allowed to be present nor to be legally represented. She was not told the findings but an inspector of police read to her a military order prohibiting any marching or any kind of procession at the child's funeral—even by children.

In the town of Balina four young men who were captured by the police were shot dead.[20] The same night a drunk or mad member of the Auxiliaries held up an old woman, and accompanied her to her house where he met the old woman's husband. The Auxiliary handed him his pistol and asked the old man to shoot him in the stomach. The old man refused the offer so the Auxiliary took his pistol back and threatened to shoot the old man for being so unco-operative. Eventually, however, he just wandered off, grumbling about the "bloody Irish".

Collins was deeply conscious of the sufferings of his own people, but he clearly realized that the terror must go on. With few men and little ammunition he knew that he could not defeat the British by force, but he could and would defeat them through their conduct.

Writing about the peace conferences with Britain after the Truce with the British Government of 1921, Collins said: "As we had almost reached the peak of our endeavour; world opinion regarding us was being forced on Britain. She had to recognize the fact. The terror which she created could not go on. It was never a success probably because it was mishandled. The idea of mixing Irish police, British ex-Officers, the Military, the Black and Tans would never work. It was probably the most quarrelsome force/forces ever to exist. Segregated by us, the R I C became a spent force—our pressure made it so. The Auxiliaries were little more than soldiers of fortune. The Black and Tans a motley, lawless crowd. But the great danger was always the military, probably because they chose to remain almost aloof from their mixed partners.

"Friction and stupidity have been the main cause of the British losing foothold in Ireland. We applied the pressure in the proper places. . . . World opinion has forced them to take the step of these conferences. They want to clear their name with the World."

That was written in 1921, but in 1920 the great danger to Collins's organization was the military intelligence and murder machine. If they succeeded in breaking the Dublin organization of the I R A the whole movement would disintegrate. The fighting would go on, no doubt, hopelessly—but fighting was not enough. It was the calculated, carefully controlled, well aimed, and vehemently prosecuted campaign brilliantly directed by Collins and his immediate assistants that was vital. The gun was necessary but futile without the pen.

The military intelligence, playing a desperate and bloody game of blind-man's-buff, stumbled at times near the heart of the Collins organization. Their activities during the dark curfew hours in Dublin might uncover the very centre of the Irish conspiracy, and wreck the complete organization.

On one night raid they disturbed Collins's deputy, who managed to escape by the skin of his teeth, leaving his documents behind. On another occasion they quizzed the editor of the *Irish Bulletin* and nearly shot him, but decided that he was not dangerous—perhaps because, as one of them put it, "We have no time for fellows who won't have their hair cut." [21]

The Dublin District Special Branch of the British Intelligence consisted almost completely of ex-officers, who were trained at a school in London and made their way singly to Dublin, where they obtained all types of "cover" jobs. One worked as a shop assistant, another as a garage hand and the rest in any kind of job they could get. They picked up items of information which they sent direct to London as it was not safe to send it to Dublin Castle. Through members of the I R A intelligence working in the British Intelligence units, some of them were discovered and shot. But these men did

E

not constitute a great menace as the ordinary people with whom they came in contact knew little or nothing about the inner workings of the I R A, and at that time, anyway, the Irish people were very careful about what they said to strangers or to people whom they did not know well.

Each British Army Command had its own Intelligence Unit, but these units had no contacts amongst the ordinary people and were quite useless. The R I C who used to be the most efficient of all intelligence units were rendered harmless, and the "G" Division of the Dublin Metropolitan Police, having been deprived by shooting of all their vicious sleuths, were to all intents and purposes working for the I R A.

Sir Nevil Macready and Sir Ormonde Winter—who became known in Ireland as the "Holy Terror", because he was always prepared to descend to the most extreme methods to obtain information from prisoners—urged the formation of a new intelligence force of experienced and ruthless men. Such a force was recruited and it included men who had served in a similar capacity in Egypt and in Russia with the Army.

There can be no doubting the courage of these men who volunteered for dangerous duty in a dangerous capital. Neither can there be any doubt of the stupidity of the men who sent them to their deaths. Nobody could convince Sir Henry Wilson, then the Chief of the Imperial General Staff, that the I R A were anything but a murdering gang of morons—"rats" and "assassins" he called them. He failed to appreciate either the brains or the purpose behind the I R A. He never guessed, or perhaps wouldn't accept, that his own intelligence organizations were riddled with Sinn Fein spies, and his approval of the recruiting of the new force is typical of the man who did not agree with unofficial reprisals but advocated official ones and the shooting by roster of Sinn Fein leaders.

These men of the "Cairo Gang", as they were referred to by some of Collins's men, were not all murderers themselves, but their experience and cleverness constituted a grave risk to the I R A. They were given access to all and any information that might exist in the files at Dublin Castle, and their arrival in Dublin meant that late night raids and interrogations were now being carried out by men of different calibre from drunken Auxiliaries and dim-witted Black and Tans. McLean, the Chief Intelligence Officer, courteously interrogated James Fleming after the escape of Breen and Tracey, even to offering his prisoner Egyptian cigarettes before letting him walk out.

Collins received information from a contact in Scotland Yard that this group of men were coming to Dublin, with the avowed intention of smashing the Dublin I R A organization, and that they had full authority to use any methods they chose, including murder. They, above the Law, entered into combat with the I R A who were beyond the Law. The secret weapon of the British was poised against the secret organization of the Irish. "Those fellows," said Collins, "were going to put a lot of us on the spot."

Collins was Director of I R A Intelligence in addition to all his other duties, and he alone dealt with many of his contacts. His Deputy Director of Intelligence was Liam Tobin, whose offices were within 200 yards of Dublin Castle. Another section of the I R A Intelligence was headed by Eamonn Duggan, a Dublin solicitor, whose offices looked across at the walls of Dublin Castle. Rows of law books and legal documents hid data, papers and records dealing with the work of his intelligence department.

The special squad known as the "Twelve Apostles" acted as detectives, shadowing suspects, known informers and the touts who were acting as look-out men for members of the British undercover agents. The "Twelve Apostles" were also fearless and experienced gunmen who, when the identity of a spy was confirmed, acted as executioners. Cathal Brugha, the Chief of Staff of the I R A, was responsible for sanctioning executions. The son of an English father and an Irish mother, Cathal was an intrepid and fearless man himself. He had been repeatedly wounded in the G P O in the rebellion of 1916 but had continued to fight and issue orders from his stretcher. He was also a very religious man who sifted the evidence against alleged spies with the most discerning integrity. Indeed, his reluctance to approve executions without the most well authenticated evidence nearly led to the I R A being hoist by their own petard on Bloody Sunday morning.

Once Collins realized the serious threat the "Cairo Gang" constituted to the lives of the leaders of the I R A and to the movement generally, he gave orders that they were to be found at their addresses, watched, and reported upon. These British intelligence men worked at night after curfew time, the period when ordinary citizens were off the streets and only members of the Dublin Metropolitan Police and the various forces of the Crown were free to roam the city. The houses which showed any activity during the hours of curfew were dangerous houses, and men who, wearing civilian clothes, walked freely through the armed patrols of Auxiliaries and Black and Tans were dangerous men.

All these houses were watched and reported upon to Collins by the unarmed members of the Dublin Metropolitan Police, who also provided professional descriptions of the groups of civilians who worked after dark—civilians who were making their final preparations for a climax as sudden and as horrifying as the one that struck them. The "Cairo Gang" knew the names of the principal sympathisers of Sinn Fein and the dossier they were building up throughout the months of October and November also included people whom they suspected but could not be sure about.

The probings of this British force and the building up of evidence by the Irish force became a dreadful contest that could only end in disaster and death for one or the other. In Cork City the British had struck first, and in Limerick City and Co. Tipperary too it was the British guns that had exploded first at the doorsteps and in the bedrooms of I R A sympathisers.

In Dublin both sides prepared.

A maid in Dublin told her boy friend about the Englishmen in her boarding house.[22] They puzzled her because they slept during the day and went out every night. She was puzzled also because they did not dress like soldiers. The boy friend was a member of the Dublin Brigade I R A and he passed this information on, and was instructed to obtain any further news he could. He asked the maid about papers left lying about the rooms occupied by these particular men, but she could not help him much. She did, however, agree to hoard all the papers from their waste-paper basket. She handed over the scraps, which were pieced together and scrutinized in the rooms overlooking the Castle.

It is as easy to pick out an Englishman in Dublin as it is to pick out an Irishman in London, and this fact in itself reflects sadly on the "brains" who sent such a squad of men for such a purpose to the Irish capital. There were Englishmen in Ireland who were there on legitimate business and not one of these men was ever interfered with by the I R A, although one of them had a narrow escape.

He bore a striking resemblance to a much sought-after

British Intelligence officer, who had been responsible for murders throughout the country. The innocent Englishman on a trip from London happened to stay in a hotel that the other one had sometimes used, and so one afternoon he answered a knock on his bedroom door to find himself facing a couple of armed and very determined young men. Luckily they were not quite sure of his identity as they did not think the agent would be so foolhardy as to use this hotel again and so on this occasion questions were asked first as a precaution. The terrified businessman showed all his papers and other documents and was able to satisfy the men of his true identity. with a brief word of apology the armed men left.

But Englishmen who went out after dark, even though they professed to be travellers, writers, or engineers, aroused curiosity, if not definite suspicion. Maids in other boarding houses were also approached by members of the I R A and much valuable information was obtained concerning the movements, correspondence and habits of the British Intelligence officers.

The evidence built up, and sometimes it was the most direct evidence. On November 14th, Tobin, the Deputy Director of Intelligence, and his assistant Thomas Cullen were sleeping at Vaughan's Hotel in Parnell Square, when a gang of the midnight marauders swooped. Face to face now, Tobin and Cullen saw some of the very men they were searching for. Tobin particularly recognized two called Bennett and Ames.

They questioned Tobin and Cullen but could not break the excellent cover story that the men had built up. The British party did not hurry, they questioned and re-questioned; but after nearly two hours they declared themselves assured—and turned to discussing race horses. During all the trouble in Ireland racing went on and race courses were recognized as

Tom Tiddler's grounds outside politics and violence.

Cullen, who was a racing fan, gave the interested officer some very good tips and they parted the best of friends. Four nights later the same group of men called at the hotel. This time they were in no chatting mood. Grimly they asked for Tobin and Cullen by name. They had found out their mistake and now they meant business. But Tobin and Cullen, in their prudence, were not chancing Vaughan's any more and slept elsewhere.

Another man who worked in the Collins Intelligence department under Tobin was Frank Thornton, and he had an even closer escape. He was picked up, held for ten days and questioned by several of the group. He stuck to his cover story and was released—only to return immediately to his department with detailed descriptions of the British undercover men.

A list of thirty-five names, addresses, descriptions and, where possible, photographs was eventually drawn up, and thirty-five portfolios giving detailed accounts of these agents' activities accompanied the list. They were not all Englishmen and they were not all members of the "Cairo Gang", but all of them were deeply involved in and familiar with the aims and objects of that particular group of the British Intelligence.

Cathal Brugha carefully and methodically went through the list and made his recommendations—in fifteen of the cases he was not convinced. This list, with Brugha's recommendations, was passed to the Cabinet of the I R A. They, too, carefully considered the evidence concerning each man. They accepted Brugha's recommendations and fifteen names were struck out.

Then Collins contacted his troops. The Commander of the Dublin Brigade, the Brigade which was the first line of defence of the Irish Government, was Richard McKee, a handsome dark-haired man and experienced soldier, who worked as a printer when not engaged in fighting. At this time there were no paid members of the I R A, they were all spare-time soldiers. On the 17th of November Michael Collins sent a note to McKee informing him that he had definitely established the addresses of the British spies, whom he referred to in the note as the "particular ones". In the note also he wrote that "Lt.G." suggested the 21st and he ordered McKee to make the necessary arrangements.

"Lieutenant G." was a member of Collins's Intelligence service who was serving with the British Army. He was known only to Collins and a few others of the Dublin leaders, and his information from inside was one of the most important pieces of evidence that sealed the fate of the "Cairo Group". Collins accepted his advice to carry out the executions on Sunday 21st because Lt. G. was in a position to forecast accurately that most of the "wanted" men would be at their addresses on that date.

There were now only four days to go. McKee informed his deputy and friend Peadar Clancy of the importance, extent and purpose of Sunday morning's operations, and together they arranged the details. Members of the "Twelve Apostles" who had an intimate knowledge of the districts where the condemned men lived, and also of the interior lay-outs of the houses, would be accompanied on their grim task and "covered" by members of the Dublin battalions.

The "Twelve Apostles" had left little to chance. Many of them had already been in the houses and found out the rooms where the British officers slept, having gained access in the guise of plumbers, gas-men, or telephone engineers. Keys to bedrooms had been obtained in some cases.

By Saturday night, picked men from each company of the

Dublin Brigade had been instructed to muster at appointed places in the city by 8.45 a.m. on Sunday morning. Other members of the I R A from outlying parts of the city had also been instructed to take up positions where they would act as reserve "cover" parties for the groups who were to visit the houses.

Nothing that could be provided for was left to chance, but one thing could not be provided for—the hit and miss tactics of the police. In spite of all the careful planning, the arrangements were almost completely wrecked by the Auxiliaries on Saturday night. Indeed, had the Auxiliaries been a few minutes earlier on this particular raid they would have captured Collins himself.

In order to make a personal report on the arrangements and to finalize details, McKee and Clancy met Collins in Vaughan's Hotel on Saturday night. It may seem foolhardy to meet in a hotel which was known to the British as a place used by the rebel leaders, but there were many things to recommend it to the I R A. The proprietor and staff were known and trusted, the various exits and hiding places were known, and it was conveniently placed in the city.

One night the Auxiliaries had raided the place and, finding nobody else, whisked the waiter, Christy, off to the Castle, where he was interviewed by an intelligence officer, who told him that they were suspicious about the hotel. This officer suggested to Christy that the next time Collins visited there Christy should slip out to a telephone and call the Castle. He promised the waiter a large sum of money and a safe passage out of the country in return. Christy agreed to the officer's terms and returned to the hotel, where he told Collins all about it. As the poet Seamus O'Sullivan said afterwards to Cathal O'Shannon: "Sure if Christy ever earned the money—

it would be the same as if he changed his name to Christy Eleison."

It was busy at Vaughan's on that Saturday night and it may well be that some tout tipped off the Castle about the activity. McKee and Clancy saw various other people who would be busy on Sunday morning, and checked with them the meeting places, addresses and procedure. After a final word with Collins they left as it was approaching curfew time. They had to deliver one more message to a squad leader concerning two of the condemned British officers, who had chosen that very night to change their address. This so delayed them that in order to get off the streets by curfew they had to hurry to a safe house, Fitzpatrick's in Cloucester Street, which was nearby.

A young man named Clune had arrived in Dublin that day, with his employer. He was very anxious to meet Mr Piaras Beaslai, who had led the party which occupied the Four Courts in 1916, and who was editor of the Republican paper *An-t-Oglach* and a leading member of the I R A. He was also a pioneer in matters affecting the Gaelic League in which Clune was deeply interested; but Clune had no knowledge of matters affecting the I R A. Clune was taken to Vaughan's Hotel to meet Beaslai by a mutual friend and both men remained to chat after the I R A leaders left.

They were deep in conversation when a friend of Beaslai's walked in to tell him that the Auxiliaries had surrounded the place and were about to raid. Piaras, who was a much wanted man, immediately went through an exit he knew into the yard where he hid in an outhouse. Clune, who knew nothing about the I R A and had nothing to fear, remained in the room.

Piaras spent an uncomfortable night in the outhouse. It would not be safe to venture back to the hotel because the

Auxiliaries had a habit of pouncing back in the hope of catching the unwary. When he looked in next morning he was told that the police had taken young Clune with them, but this did not worry Piaras because he knew him to be completely ignorant of I R A matters.

Collins, when he left the hotel that night, went to another favourite meeting place of the leaders, a bar in the Gaiety Theatre, which was also the meeting place of British officers off duty and British loyalists. "It had," said one of the I R A, "a respectable air of legal and loyal comfort—no one would expect a republican to pollute its atmosphere."

A military police sergeant lived just off Gloucester Street to which McKee and Clancy had repaired. This man was suspected by the I R A of giving information to the Castle and some members of the I R A had asked previously for permission to eliminate him. This had been refused because there was not sufficient evidence.

Circumstances, however, clearly suggest that on this Saturday night he watched the two men enter Fitzpatrick's and phoned this information to the Castle. At 2 a.m. McKee and Clancy were awakened by the sound of screaming tyres, clanging doors and shouts as a party of Auxiliaries rushed to and broke down Fitzpatrick's front door.

McKee quickly pulled all his papers out of his pockets and lit them in the grate—amongst them the list of the officers who were to die next morning. Hardly had the papers been destroyed when the Auxiliaries were pounding at the door. The door was opened and McKee, Clancy and the landlord, Fitzpatrick, were given a few minutes to dress, bundled into the lorry, driven off to Dublin Castle and thrust into a room where they met Clune for the first time.

The two key men of Bloody Sunday had been captured!

THE PASSING OF ''THE PARTICULAR ONES''

BLOODY SUNDAY morning was mild. A wintry sun shone on the streets of Dublin, the forces of the Crown who had been patrolling the streets during the hours of curfew had retired. There were many people in the streets hurrying as the bells of the several churches reminded them that nine o'clock mass would soon begin. In the hurrying crowds were young men in trench coats, but they were not going towards the crowded churches, they were timing their arrivals at their various assignments, trying not to be too soon and fearing that they might be too late.

As the bells were still ringing the groups met and at three minutes to the hour they moved.[1]

The first shots fired that morning were fired at a shadow.[2] Three men moved up the stairs of the Shelbourne Hotel. The leading man held his automatic pistol at the ready and, as he turned a corner of the stairs, looked up to see a figure coming towards him—and the man approaching him had an automatic pistol jutting out steadily. The I R A man fired a burst and saw the mirror he was approaching, shatter. Upstairs, a British agent heard the shots and reacted quickly. Picking up his revolver, he fled from his room and up into the higher regions of the hotel. The need for secrecy gone, the three I R A ran to the room where they expected to find their target, but it was empty and the hotel too large to search quickly. They hurriedly thrust papers they found lying about into their pockets and retraced their footsteps to the front door.

No. 28 Upper Pembroke Street was a popular rambling old boarding house managed by a silvery-haired matronly woman named Mrs Grey. She had many boarders, most of them military officers, and a staff of maids and a porter to serve their wants. Recently, a man from the plumber's had examined pipes in the house and had been shown around by one of the maids. Afterwards Mrs Grey remembered that she had forgotten to ask who had sent for him. Mrs Grey had not noticed anything peculiar about her boarders, but her maids had.

Two of them in particular. A maid noticed that they used to leave the house after dark—after curfew—and used to sleep late during the day. They were soldiers, because the maid saw their uniforms hanging in the cupboards, but when they went out at nights they used to wear ordinary clothes. Mr Dowling and Mr Price were strange ones all right! Most of the other boarders were British officers, nice polite gentlemen, Rosie thought, but they always wore uniform and slept through the night when they were off duty.

Rosie was up early on Sunday morning because she had to have the breakfasts ready by 9 a.m. Matt, the porter, was down in the hall polishing the lino and the cook was in the kitchen preparing breakfast—the pleasant aroma of toast mixed in Matt's nostrils with the smell of lino polish and he was wondering, as he polished, about Dublin's chances in the big football match that afternoon at Croke Park. He heard the bells ringing for nine o'clock mass but he was not interested—he had already been at eight o'clock mass.

And now just as the bells stopped there came a sharp knock at the front door. He climbed slowly to his feet. He was used to these sharp knocks—it was probably a letter for one of the officers—sharp knocks were commonplace nowadays. As he turned the knob on the lock, the door was knocked out of his hand and he was pushed against the wall, to stare into the eyes of a man pointing a revolver at him. And as the man stood there other men passed quickly behind him into the hall. There were about nine of them and they followed the leader up the stairs whilst one or two other men stood about in the hall, and one went through to the back of the house. They all had revolvers or pistols and Matt just stood there wondering what was going to happen next.

Upstairs, Mrs Grey was just leaving her room when she saw men coming up the stairs. The leading one motioned with his gun and said, "Get in your room," and as she did so they passed on.

Major Dowling, an officer of the Grenadier Guards, and Captain Leonard Price, M.C.—he had been decorated for gallantry in the field—of the General List of Officers previously of the Middlesex Regiment, occupied adjoining rooms on the third floor. Now they were fully dressed and about to go down to breakfast. They were both in uniform on this morning.

The other officers in the house were moving about in their rooms as well. Captain H. B. C. Keenlyside, M.C., and his wife were in a room on the second floor where Colonel Wood-cock, D.S.O., also had a room. On the first floor Colonel Montgomery and Lieutenant Murray of the Royal Scots had rooms. Keenlyside, Woodcock and Montgomery were all officers of the 1st Battalion the Lancashire Fusiliers.

The I R A men reached the third floor. One of them tapped on Colonel Dowling's door and another officer in the house heard a high-pitched voice—he thought it was a girl's voice—say, "I have a letter for you, sir." Almost immediately the silence of the house was broken by the sharp bark of automatic pistols—two bursts that merged and echoed together.

Shots that brought all the other officers to their doors—none of them armed. Colonel Woodcock saw a youth with a gun on the stairs. The youth said, "Put your hands up." Woodcock heard a shout from Montgomery, "Get your gun!" Woodcock turned to go back to his room, the youth fired and he fell by the door with a bullet in his back.

Shots echoed now all over the house. Lieutenant Murray had run downstairs to the hall where he was held up by the I R A men posted there. Colonel Montgomery on the first floor opened his door and was immediately shot down. Upstairs, Captain Keenlyside was joined on the landing by his wife. Three I R A told her to get out of it but she ran close to her husband and fought when they tried to pull her off. Then one, seeing his opportunity, fired and hit Keenlyside in the arm, and the men ran downstairs. In the room where Dowling lay dead the leader of the intruders said to one of his men who was searching the room for papers, "Come on. Get out of it quickly. Go on. Get out." The young man ran downstairs, past the bodies of the officers and past where Lieutenant Murray was being held in the hall. "I felt a great pang of pity for the officers," said the man afterwards. "And especially for the man in the hall who was about to be shot."

But the killings and shootings had shattered the men of the execution squad—the advent of a struggling woman had made it all the more horrible, and the unexpected appearance of officers from almost every doorway had strained to breaking point their already fraught nerves. They fired at Murray and left him where he fell, but they did not kill him.

The house was like an abattoir. When the I R A men left, Mrs Grey and the maid ran upstairs to find Major Dowling and Captain Price dead and Mrs Keenlyside comforting her wounded and bloody husband. They found an officer on the second floor crawling into his room, another unconscious by his door and Lieutenant Murray stunned in the hall.

The young man whose duty it had been to search the rooms of the dead officers hurried to where a boat would carry him across the river, for Dublin is surrounded by bridges which the British manned and barred when there was trouble about. He caught his ferry boat and after putting away his gun was in time for twelve o'clock mass.

And later on the maid who had told her boy friend about the men who went out after dark saw him again and, bursting into tears, said: "Oh, why did you do that to them, I thought you would only kidnap them and send them away."

Lieutenant D. L. McLean of the General List, late of the Rifle Brigade and now Chief Intelligence Officer, lived with his wife at 119 Morehampton Road. Recently, they had been joined by his wife's brother, J. Caldow from Scotland, who, it was said was hoping to join the police in Ireland through the good services of his brother-in-law. They shared the house with their friends Mr and Mrs T. H. Smith and their three children, one of them a ten-year-old boy.

It was this young boy who answered the knock on the front door and watched six men with guns in their hands hurry into the house and up to the bedrooms. McLean was in bed with his wife and he had no doubt about what was going to happen. "Not here," McLean said, "not in front of my wife." "Get upstairs," said the leader. The landlord, Mr Smith, and the brother-in-law, Caldow, were also being urged up the stairs. There was an unoccupied room up there and into it the three men were thrust—then came the sound of shots. The gunmen hurried down the stairs and out into the street, slamming the door after them. Mrs McLean ran upstairs—her husband and Smith lay dead, her brother was badly wounded. Careless of her attire in her terrible grief, she ran into the roadway where she met two policemen who went back with her to the house.

At 92 Lower Baggot Street, Captain W. F. Newbury of the Royal West Surrey Regiment lived with his wife who was shortly to have a baby. They occupied a small flat in the house. The landlady, Mrs Stack, answered the knock on the door and four men went upstairs where they knocked again. Mrs Newbury got out of bed to answer the knock, leaving the bedroom door open and walking across the living-room. She opened the door, saw the men and the guns and threw herself against the door to shut it again, but she was cast aside. She ran back to the bedroom, her body covering her husband who was standing by the bedroom door in his pyjamas. They both entered the bedroom and slammed the door, but the men had now reached it. The Newburys pushed hard and nearly closed it when a shot was fired through the door and Newbury staggered back. Turning he ran, spitting blood, to the window which was open, and had climbed half-way through when the men entered. They pushed the wife to one side and as he straddled the window-ledge they fired a burst into him and he slumped dead. As the shooting was going on other men were searching, hurriedly stuffing papers and notebooks into their pockets. The leader gave an order and they left. Mrs Newbury pathetically placed a blanket across the body of her husband. A week afterwards her baby arrived—stillborn.

Lieutenant Peter Ashmunt Ames, late of the Grenadier Guards, was the son of Mrs Eleanor Ames of Morristown, New Jersey, U.S.A. He was on the Army General List—an official designation which covers a multitude of purposes. His friend Lieutenant G. Bennett, late of the Royal Artillery, described then as being on the "special Army list", lived in a room opposite him at 38 Upper Mount Street.

George Bennett, holding the rank of Temporary Captain, was a native of Bournemouth, Hampshire. He was educated at Sherborne and at Magdalen College, Oxford, where he took Honours in Law. He had joined the Motor Transport Corps of the British Army but afterwards had been transferred to the Intelligence Corps, which brought him in touch with many regiments. After being demobilized from the Army he was approached and asked to join the Intelligence again for work in Ireland. He was one of the hard core of the "Cairo Gang".

Katherine Farrell, the maid who answered the knock on the door, was asked by the first man, "Is Mr Ames in?" "Yes," she replied. The man with the gun motioned her up the stairs in front of him and when they came to Bennett's room he told her to go up the next stairs. The men entered Bennett's room and ordered him out of bed. They crossed the corridor with him and pushed him in front of them into the room occupied by Ames, who was now ordered out of bed. Then the shooting started and they fell dead together. The I R A withdrew and the maid ran downstairs with another officer. They found only the corpses.

Captain Fitzgerald lived in a boarding house at 28 Earls-fort Terrace. He was an Irishman, the son of a Tipperary doctor. He was employed as a Barracks Defence Officer in Co. Clare, where some time before he had been kidnapped by a body of I R A men. They took his own revolver and held it to his head, but, when they pulled the trigger, it misfired. They pushed him into a field and in the struggle his arm had been dislocated. Propping him against a wall, they again pointed the revolver at his head and pulled the trigger. This time it did not misfire but the bullet missed his head. He dropped to the ground and pretended to be dead—they took it for granted that he was. When they left he made his way back to barracks. He had been sent to Dublin for treatment for his dislocated arm, had been discharged after a period in hospital and was sleeping peacefully on this Sunday morning when the executioners knocked at the front door.

"Is Mr Fitzpatrick in?" asked the leader of the armed men. "He is a lieutenant-colonel," he explained. "There is no Mr Fitzpatrick here," said the maid, "only a Captain Fitzgerald." "Show us his room," said the leader and the girl led them to Captain Fitzgerald's room. As she stood outside two men went in. She heard one of them say, "Come on." The captain screamed, revolver shots drowned and silenced his cries. The men went away after searching the room for papers.

The police found two bullets had passed through his head, one through his heart and one through the hand which he had held up to protect himself.

That morning at the Gresham Hotel, in O'Connell Street, Captain McCormack of the Royal Army Veterinary Corps, was sitting up in bed reading Sunday newspapers in room No. 22, and in Room 14 Mr A. L. Wilde was sleeping. Captain McCormack had, indeed, come from Egypt, but not to serve with the Military Intelligence, only to buy mules for the Army. Three days previously Wilde[2] had written a letter to Arthur Henderson of the British Labour Party which was published in the newspapers on Monday, 22 November, begging him to put the writer in touch with people who could help him to dedicate his life to fighting for democracy. In it he wrote that he had had many discussions with the Catholic clergy and that he deplored the state of affairs then existing in Ireland.

Downstairs, Hugh Gallagher, the doorman, was standing near the hotel entrance ready to receive guests. He politely held the door open as a group of men carrying pistols and revolvers approached. The leader asked Hugh to conduct them to Rooms Nos. 14 and 24. One of the men was carrying a sledge-hammer but not, as the Chief Secretary for Ireland reported afterwards, to finish off their victims but for the more reasonable task of shattering the locks of the hotel doors, if that became necessary. In the event the sledge-hammer was not used for either purpose. When the men tapped at No. 14, Wilde opened the door and immediately received three bullets through the chest and heart.

Following Hugh Gallagher, the party then went to No. 22— not No. 24 as asked for. The door was unlocked. They opened it and fired five bullets through the unfortunate Captain McCormack, who died immediatey.

Lieutenant "Angliss" and his Irish colleague, Lieutenant "Peel", occupied rooms facing one another on the first floor of No. 22 Lower Mount Street. Angliss's real name was McMahon, and he was one of the men recalled from Russia to organize the intelligence group working in the South Dublin area. An experienced intelligence officer, he had noticed that the I R A were trailing him and he had warned Peel to be extra careful. A few days previously McMahon had escaped death when a party of I R A entered a billiards saloon, which he frequented, in order to shoot him. When they entered he was upstairs having a cup of tea with the proprietor and so was undetected.

Once again as the church bells ceased their tolling the door knocker was rapped, and the girl who opened it was told peremptorily to show them where Lieutenant Angliss slept. She led them up the stairs and pointed. They entered the room and fired five times at McMahon as he lay in bed, killing him. Then the leader asked where Peel slept. The terrified girl pointed at another bedroom door. But Peel, hearing the shots, had piled furniture against the door. They tried to burst it down but the door was firm. They fired wildly through the door, about twenty holes were found in it afterwards, but they missed Peel. Then a new sound was heard—rifle shots in the street and a cry of alarm from the men who had been left to guard the hall: "The Auxiliaries are outside."

A lorry load of Auxiliaries had been passing on its way to the station. As they drove through Lower Mount Street they saw, rather than heard, a maid screaming from the top window of the house. The lorry stopped and they heard the sounds of the shots within the house. Unhesitantly they rushed the door. It was slammed in their faces. Some of them ran round to the back of the house through a narrow lane nearby, and the officer in charge ordered two of them to return to barracks to get help. These two, Garner and Morris, started back at the double.

Shots were now coming from the house. The I R A divided into two parties. One went through the back door to the lane; the other, led by Tom Keogh, opened the front door again and came out shooting. One of the I R A men was hit in the arm in the exchange of shots and was supported by two companions. Still firing, they retreated and vanished.

At the back the Auxiliaries saw the men retreating and opened fire. One shot hit Frank Teeling, of the I R A, in the ankle and he fell crippled. The others disappeared.

The two Auxiliaries on their way to get more help from Beggars Bush Barracks—a few hundred yards away—ran into the covering force of I R A, near Mount Street Bridge. They were taken into a garden and shot dead.

A military motor-cyclist witnessed the battle and drove to the barracks to alert the Auxiliaries, who were at that moment being inspected by their Commanding Officer, Brigadier-General Crozier. They immediately boarded lorries and drove quickly to the scene, where they found the same lady hanging out of the same window still screaming.

There was no trace of the I R A to be seen until Crozier rushed through the house into the back, and there on the ground was Teeling with an Auxiliary beside him, and the Auxiliary had his revolver against Teeling's forehead and was counting up to ten. He had been questioning the I R A man, asking him the names of his companions, but Teeling had refused to talk. Now the Auxiliary was giving him his last chance. Crozier knocked the revolver up and ordered one of his officers to arrange for Teeling to be sent to hospital under guard. Then Crozier went upstairs in the house. He found McMahon dead in a blood-soaked bed and Peel's door still bolted. He persuaded Peel that it was all right and the door was opened to reveal a very scared and trembling man—but a man who recovered quickly because he was on another intelligence raid the same night.[3]

At 119 Lower Baggot Street, Captain G. T. Bagally, one-legged barrister and Courts-Martial Officer, lived in his room. A native of Wimbledon, London, he had lost his leg on active service. He was well known as a redoubtable prosecutor of the I R A and had been involved in the murder of an innocent businessman named Lynch in a hotel in Dublin. McMahon had been one of the men in on the shooting of Lynch, whom they probably mistook for General Liam Lynch, Commander of the First Southern Division of the I R A—the man who had captured and overcome General Lucas. They shot Lynch, the businessman, as he lay in bed. Bagally's part in this murder had not been great but he had co-operated in sending police cars to the hotel—enough to condemn him as being in the confidence of the men who had perpetrated it. Five bullets were pumped into his body. When the police found him there was no other person in the house. The following day the chair-man of a resumed court-martial on an I R A man, Michael O'Rourke, accused of killing a British soldier, Private Rogers, mentioned the death of Captain Bagally who had been en-gaged in the case and extended sympathy to his relatives.

In other parts of the city execution parties called, but did not find their quarry. Colonel Jennings was not in the East-wood Hotel when they arrived. Nor were the officers asked for at the Standard Hotel in residence that morning. One officer who should have been at home spent the night, it was after-wards discovered, with a lady in a more disreputable part of the city.

Captain Crawford of the Royal Army Service Corps was in bed with his wife at their flat in Fitzwilliam Square when there came a tap on his door. Thinking it was one of his men with a message, he called out, "Come in," but nobody entered. He opened the door to find three men with pointing revolvers who stepped into the room. "Put your hands up," said one of them. "Is this a joke?" he asked and kept his hands down. "It's no joke—are you Major Callaghan?" said the man, sticking his gun in the Captain's stomach while Mrs Crawford watched from the bed. "There is a Mr Callaghan living upstairs but he is not in the Army and has no connection with the Army," said Captain Crawford. They asked him many questions. He told them he was in charge of the Motor Repair Department. "Why the hell do you come here? Why don't you mind your own business in England?" asked one of the men. The leader said, "You are telling us damn' lies—you are in the secret service. Show me your papers."

They ordered him back into bed with his wife and, as one of the armed party stood over them the rest examined the room thoroughly. They opened every drawer and scrutinized every scrap of paper. Eventually they seemed satisfied, but suddenly one of them turned to the Captain again and said, "Get out," and he got out of bed again.

The Captain was now sure that they were going to shoot him. He said, "My wife is not very well. If you are going to shoot me please take me downstairs—it would be most unpleasant for her." "Shut up," said the leader. "Why should this happen to me—what have I done to deserve this?" said Mrs Crawford. "You shut up, too," said the leader. The two men who had been searching the room upstairs now came down and the men left; as they did the leader called out, "You bloody well clear out of this country in twenty hours or we will come back tomorrow night and do for you."

At the same time in another part of the city James Kenny, whom the over-enthusiastic Dutchman had accidentally shot in the rebel headquarters at the G P O in 1916 was hurrying away from a house with a group of colleagues. They had drawn a blank—their target was not at home.[4]

James, at this time a lieutenant in the 4th Dublin Battalion, had been warned on Saturday to make ready for an important operation to take place on Sunday. He was advised to go to confession—a sure sign that there was going to be a good element of personal danger—and to join a colleague, Frank Burke, a schoolmaster. Neither of them was to sleep at his own home on Saturday night.

They went instead to a boarding house which James knew, and were up bright and early on Sunday morning and at the appointed place on time. They were joined there by eight other men including two who were strangers to James. These two were the experts, toughened and efficient at the bloody business of killing in cold blood; they were two of the "Twelve Apostles".

At the house of their choice everything went according to plan. James hurried, as instructed, to the back, to block off any escape route in that direction. Others took up covering positions at doors and the corners of corridors. The two executioners burst open the door of the officer's room, only to find a very scared and rather ashamed lady in one half of a double bed. The officer had not been there that night, she did not know why. She had expected him.

At about the same time young Eileen Horan was hurrying home to her mother's high-class boarding house near St Stephen's Green. She saw a group of young men come out of the house and scatter. She found her mother in the hall flustered and very irate. "They came to shoot Mr Cleveden, the civil servant. They ought to be ashamed of themselves, he is such a nice young man. Luckily he did not come in last night," said her mother, who continued to grumble until the following Tuesday.[5]

On Tuesday an armoured car and a lorry load of Auxiliaries crashed to a halt outside her front door and "Mr Cleveden", now in the uniform of a British officer and neither civil nor friendly, walked into the house with an escort. He packed up his clothes and left without a word. Mrs Horan was furious to find out that she had been taken in by a spy, especially by one who had left without paying.

She wrote to the Commanding Officer of the military complaining at the deception, and asking for the money due to her, but he did not even trouble to reply.

Fifteen officers of the British intelligence had been sentenced by the legally elected Government of the Irish people, and condemned to die on that morning. Eleven of them were killed and four officers wounded. Two "cadets" of the Auxiliaries had been shot dead and the officer of the Royal Army

Veterinary Corps, Captain McCormack, had been killed in the tragic mistake at the Gresham Hotel. Amongst the four who escaped were the Lieutenant-Colonel in charge of the "Cairo Gang", Mr "Peel" who had successfully barricaded himself in his room, and the agent who had disappeared into the upper regions of the Shelbourne Hotel when the I R A had fired at his own reflection in the mirror.

9

MASSACRE BY THE BLACK AND TANS

GENERAL CROZIER, after arranging for the transference of Frank Teeling, the wounded I R A man, to hospital and the removal also of his own two dead Auxiliaries—they had been killed because they would subsequently be able to recognize their captors if allowed to live—drove to Dublin Castle. He found most of his colleagues there having breakfast. In his own book, *Ireland for Ever*, he describes, with a certain air of light relief, how he shocked them and spoiled their breakfasts by describing the scene he had just left.

Whilst he was there further reports of deaths arrived by telephone and he heard a staggered officer say, "About fifty officers have been shot. Collins has done in most of the secret service people."

He was quite unruffled by the events of the morning and played squash and had a hot bath before going on for lunch to the Shelbourne Hotel where he stared at, and puzzled over, the bullet-shattered mirror before sitting down to dine with a Liberal Member of Parliament. The M P had come to Ireland to have first-hand experience of the terror which the British forces were handing out! Crozier wrote about this lunch: "We were in the midst of cheery fellows, chaffing, laughing and speculating as to what the politicians would be like in Westminster next day as, in safety looking down their noses with their chins in the air, they would stamp the floor in anger and call the 'shinners' every name under the sun. . . ."

Next day, in fact, they did just that but added a sensational free-for-all on the floor of the House of Commons.

As General Crozier and his friends were wining and dining, men, women and children were trooping to the sports stadium at Croke Park, a few miles away, for what was advertised as "G.A.A. CHALLENGE MATCH. FOOTBALL. Tipperary (Challengers) v. Dublin (Leinster Champions) AN ALL-IRELAND TEST at Croke Park on the 21st inst. at 2-45 p.m. A THRILLING GAME EXPECTED."

And a thrilling game it turned out to be. It had been well advertised and well organized. The money raised from the match was to help the Association for the dependants of the I R A who had been killed or imprisoned. Jack Shouldice was on the Committee—representing the Dublin Brigade, which had arranged the match some weeks before. He was in charge that day of the gate and field arrangements, and was reasonably happy as the ground began to fill. Outside and surrounding the ground were the ticket sellers—they sold from a roll of paper tickets and admittance was gained by producing one of these tickets at the gates. These ticket sellers were spaced at fairly even intervals around the ground and about thirty yards from it.[1]

The organizers were worried as more and more news arrived about the shootings of the British intelligence men in various parts of the city. They were even more apprehensive when officers from the Dublin Brigade I R A arrived and advised them either to cancel or postpone the match, in case the British should start anything. The officials discussed the position and in the end decided to go ahead with the arrangements. Their main reason was that if they cancelled the match the British would identify the Gaelic Athletic Association with the shootings of the early morning. Besides, the spectators and players were used to raids and searches by the Black and Tans, and there was no reason to believe that they would be responsible for anything very unpleasant happening. Surely they would not disturb a football match. All during the troubles, race meetings had continued to be held and on such occasions both sides observed an automatic truce. Amongst the officials with whom Jack Shouldice discussed the matter were Alderman Nowlan, Luke O'Toole, Andy Harty and Dan McCarthy.

The game started on time—or as near time as makes no difference in Ireland—and Mick Sammon the referee threw the ball in. This was a Challenge match and the players lost no time in going all out for victory. There were several thrilling bouts and soon the crowd had forgotten all about the cares and troubles of the rest of the island outside the walls of the football arena, and were cheering with marked partisanship the skill and courage of the players. Even an aeroplane flying low around the field did not distract their attention, nor did many of the spectators see the the red signal flare that was shot from the cockpit.

The game was in full swing when the dreaded Black and Tans appeared suddenly on top of a wall enclosing one side of the ground. They had used ladders to scale the wall and were now dropping down into the football ground. They formed up into a rough line with rifles at their shoulders, and then an officer on top of the wall fired a revolver shot. This was the signal for the first ragged volley from the police. The spectators and players were not at first alarmed and one of the football officials shouted to the startled players, "It's all right—they are only firing blanks."

The volume of rifle fire increased and the frightening clatter of sub-machine guns was added to it. It became horrifyingly clear also that it was not blank cartridges that were being fired.

Men and women slumped to the ground—the crowd panicked and fled away from the flashing muzzles. On the pitch the players dispersed—except two who lay still, one on the grass, the other half on the grass and half on the cinder track that then surrounded the field. They both wore the Tipperary colours.

The players in their distinctive jerseys now mingled with the milling crowd which piled against the wall, seeming to spill over it on the side of the ground farthest from the murdering fire of the forces of the Crown. As the crowd surged it passed over and left behind bullet-shattered and trampled bodies of men, women and children.

Bullets thudded and whistled everywhere. A little boy who had won himself a grandstand seat on the branch of a tree, tumbled to the ground and lay still, shot through the body.[2] The scene was made more noisy as machine-gun bullets ripped into the galvanized roof of the dressing-rooms in which scores of people had packed themselves for safety. An Auxiliary with a revolver in his hand ran to the door of one of these rooms and, brandishing his gun, shouted, "Here we avenge our fallen comrades." A priest gave everybody general absolution and the terrified civilians prepared for death—but the firing died away and the Black and Tans advanced into the crowd with weapons at the ready.

The thousands of terrified people still inside the ground were ordered to put their hands up and form into lines. The police passed through the ranks, frisking and calling out, "Keep your hands higher or we'll blow your bloody heads off." The Tipperary team were separated from the rest of the crowd and herded together.[3] The two Tipperary players lying on the pitch were Mick Hogan from Grangemockler and Jim Egan from Mullinahone. Jim Egan came to his feet covered in blood, walked towards the crowd and said to a priest, Father Crotty, "Mick Hogan is dead—could you go to him." It was Hogan's blood that stained Egan. The priest had his hands up and was being threatened by an Auxiliary who said: "You were not so anxious for our fellows to get the last rites when you were shooting them from behind hedges in Tipperary." But he allowed the priest to go, still with his hands up, to where Hogan was lying dead. He had been shot through the head and under the left shoulder. There was another dead man lying near Hogan, a man named Thomas Ryan from Co. Wexford. The priest did what he could for the two of them.

Ryan, one of seven brothers, had knelt by Hogan's side saying the final act of contrition into his ear when a well aimed shot killed him. They sing in Wexford:

> "Croke Park, Bloody Sunday as the dying
>   goal-man lay on the ground,
> And as the British bullets were flying round,
> Brave Thomas Ryan from Wexford fair
> Knelt by his side in dying prayer,
> And as he aided the dying man
> Was brutally shot by a Black and Tan.
> God grant that both their souls
> Find rest in Heaven among the blessed. . . ."

The searching of the crowd took a long time and it was some hours before the ground was clear. The Tipperary players were still held and corpses and seriously wounded people still littered the ground. No medical attention was allowed by the armed representatives of His Majesty's Government. It became clear that the intention of these same representatives of law and order was to execute the thirteen Tipperary players. One had escaped over the wall, one was already dead on the pitch.

A British Army officer approached the players and their captors, who stood to attention at his approach. He ordered them to stand at ease and "stand easy". Then he went amongst the players and said in a low voice, "They intend to shoot the lot of you—something must be done." He turned to the armed guards and said, "These men are in my charge. I am taking them to their hotel to search their rooms." He ordered the players to the dressing-rooms and told them to put on their overcoats, then he led them to the gate and said, "Go back to your hotel—I will follow with my men."

The Black and Tans searched the spectators rigorously but found nothing of value. They found a diary on Jack Shouldice and became suspicious of some of the entries. The officer did not examine it very closely but he ordered Shouldice to be detained with three or four others in a dressing-room for further examination later.

"After some time," Jack told me, "another Auxiliary officer came along. Most of the Black and Tans were drunk that day but this one was sober and decent. He seemed to be very upset and disgusted with the whole affair and asked why we were being detained. The armed guard handed up my diary and said that some of the entries in it appeared to require some explanation. The officer turned over the pages and asked me a few questions, which I was easily able to answer satisfactorily.

"He handed me back the book and said, 'I don't see anything worth special interrogation here. There has been enough shooting and bloodshed here today. You get away as quickly as you can.' I did not hesitate.

The men the I R A were fighting—tough, experienced veterans of World War I who formed the Auxiliaries. This company is being inspected at Beggar's Bush Barracks in Dublin.

Independent Newspapers, Dublin

The Tipperary Football Team who played against Dublin at Croke Park on Bloody Sunday. Mick Hogan (3), the player who was shot dead, stands directly in front of the second hatted figure from the left. Jim Egan (4), who fetched the priest, is the player standing on the extreme right.

Bill Lawler

"A remarkable thing was that I collected most of the gate money from the ticket sellers. Only one bag was missing. I was able to hand over £160 to the Volunteer Dependants Fund."

After the crowd had left the ground, the ambulance men arrived on their horse-drawn vehicles. One of them went about with a bucket picking up pieces of bones and a length of human thigh which had been blown from a body by the force of the point-blank bullets. They found the trampled body of Miss Jeannie Boyle, who had gone to the match with her fiancé; she was to have been married five days later. The youngest spectator to be shot was ten-year-old Jerry O'Leary. He died in his mother's arms, telling her, "Mammy, mammy, mammy, I'm shot." Eleven-year-old Willie Robinson died under the feet of the panic-stricken crowd. Fourteen-year-old J. Scott was so mutilated by a bullet that ricocheted, it was first thought he had been bayoneted to death. In all fourteen people died and sixty-two were injured, many of them seriously.

The perpetrators of this deliberate act of senseless revenge drove off, one of the lorries trailing an Irish tricolour on the ground. The Auxiliaries had excelled themselves. This Corps d'Elite was no doubt particularly enraged because two of their members—the first to die in Ireland—had been shot that morning.

Subsequently the Authorities had to explain the necessity for the massacre, and the Castle issued the following communiqué.[4]

"A number of men came to Dublin on Saturday under the guise of attending a football match between Tipperary and Dublin. But their real purpose was to act as gunmen.

"Learning on Sunday that a number of these gunmen were

F

present in Croke Park, the Crown forces went to raid the field.

"It was the original intention that an officer would go to the centre of the field and speaking from a megaphone invite the assassins to come forward. But on their approach armed pickets gave warning. Shots were fired to warn the wanted men, who caused a stampede and escaped in the confusion."

"Invite the assassins to come forward" must have caused a hearty chuckle amongst the officers and men of the Black and Tans. One of the officers of the Auxiliaries, Major Mills, stated afterwards that he heard no shots until the police opened fire. Some of the spectators were members of the I R A and carried revolvers which they very wisely dropped on the ground when it became obvious that they were to be searched. One little boy picked up an object during the rush which he hid in his pocket for inspection later. It turned out to be a detonator and blew two of his fingers off.[5] The ticket sellers, who were placed at even intervals around the ground, provided the Black and Tans with colour for their story that guards had been posted by the I R A. It was not until some years later that a high ranking officer of the Auxiliaries divulged that the Auxiliaries could not make up their minds that Sunday whether to burn and sack O'Connell Street—Dublin's main thoroughfare—or raid the football match, so they tossed up for it and Croke Park lost.

10

MURDER MOST FOUL

DICK McKEE and Peadar Clancy were thrust into the guard-room at Dublin Castle with their landlord Sean Fitzpatrick. The room was already crowded with prisoners who had been picked up in Dublin on Saturday. Many of the prisoners were active members of the I R A and their capture was one more proof of the results which the new British intelligence squad were providing. The notorious interrogator and torturer Captain Hardy and his colleague Captain King were busy that night, and later they had the expert assistance of the "holy terror", Sir Ormonde Winter, himself.

Each prisoner was interrogated separately by Hardy and his colleagues and there is little doubt that they were aware of the importance of the prisoners McKee and Clancy. The conduct of the Auxiliaries during the night was savage and tense but early on Sunday morning it became more violent and lunatic. When the news of the shootings of the officers came through to Dublin Castle the fury of the Auxiliaries knew no bounds. All the prisoners except McKee, Clancy and the innocent Clune—who the Auxiliaries believed had come to Dublin in connection with the shootings—were sent to another barracks. These three were left in the guard-room at the mercy of their infuriated captors.

MacNamara, a member of the Metropolitan detective branch who was also on Michael Collins's staff, managed to get into the Castle and have drinks with members of the

Auxiliaries in the bar next to the guard-room, but he could not approach the prisoners and he was shocked by the condition and fury of his fellow drinkers.[1] Collins had been awaiting reports on the events of the morning from McKee and Clancy when the news reached him that they had been captured. He immediately appreciated the grave position they were in and set about remobilizing the forces of the Dublin I R A to mount an open attack upon the Bridewell Barracks where he believed they were being held.

Later he was told that they were in the Castle which made such an attempt impossible. The I R A had neither the men nor the arms to carry out an attack on that impregnable fortress. About 11 a.m. on Sunday the Auxiliaries reached the pitch necessary to carry out brutal cold-blooded murder. The three defenceless prisoners were bayoneted and shot to death.

An official communiqué had to be issued in respect of their deaths.[2] The first hurriedly-prepared one stated that the three men had been killed whilst trying to escape and it described the guileless Con Clune as an officer of the Clare I R A. There had been, said the communiqué, a desperate struggle in which rifles and bombs had been used by the prisoners. They had been guarded, it said, by four members of the Auxiliaries, and three of these had left the room when the desperate men threw themselves on the remaining guard, securing rifles and bombs from a box under a bed. Then, sheltering behind mattresses, they had fired at the Auxiliaries but no Auxiliary had been wounded.

This fatuous communiqué fooled nobody, so they proceeded to bolster it up. A number of Auxiliaries posed as prisoners and others as guards for an official photographer, and these posed pictures were issued to the newspapers purporting to be actual reconstructions of the positions just before and just after the prisoners made their attempt. There had been twenty-three other prisoners in that room during the night and none of them had seen rifles or bombs—indeed, foolhardy as the Auxiliaries might have been, they would hardly have been careless enough to leave arms and ammunition lying about in the detention room.

The bombs which the I R A threw, said the communiqué, were not fused. Both McKee and Clancy knew all there was to know about hand grenades; Clune knew nothing about them. All three, however, were intelligent enough to know what would happen if a hand grenade exploded in such a confined space as that room. Such a communiqué was typical of the lawless and insulting way in which the Auxiliaries and the Authorities were treating the Irish people and misleading the people of Britain.

The bodies were handed over to relatives and they rested all night in the Catholic pro-Cathedral. The following morning Michael Collins and members of his staff attended the requiem service and helped to carry the coffins of McKee and Clancy out of the church. An enterprising photographer from the *Evening Herald* took a picture which included an excellent view of Collins. This picture appeared in an early edition of the paper and was seen by members of the I R A who realized its importance to the British authorities, who did not possess a recent picture of Michael. Every copy of the paper was collected from the newsboys on the streets and a group of I R A visited the offices of the newspaper where they smashed the photographic plate and picture block. The British intelligence heard about the picture and visited the offices half an hour afterwards.

Ben Doyle was twenty in 1920 and a very active member of the Dublin I R A. Like everybody else at that period he was a part-time soldier. It was some weeks after Bloody Sunday that Collins organized the section known as the A S U, or Active Service Unit. These men were paid a small weekly salary, just enough to pay for lodgings and food. Apart from these men the I R A, in spite of what was said in Parliament at Westminster, was an amateur army even to the men buying their own arms when they could. We have seen how near the Auxiliaries came to discovering all the I R A plans for the Sunday when they rushed in on McKee and Clancy in their room in Gloucester Street. They came even nearer than that, as Ben told me.

He was studying to be a doctor when the "troubles" started but he sacrificed his career to become an active member, and at the time was earning himself a modest income as a clerk in an insurance office. As we sat in Barry's Hotel in Dublin— the hotel where the Tipperary team stopped on the night before Bloody Sunday and which is still the usual rendezvous of football and hurling teams which visit Dublin—he told me part of his story, which he later extended and confirmed through discussions with his colleagues.

"I have never talked much about the troubles but I am now convinced that people who took an active part in them should talk about them. A kind of veil has been drawn about the period which conceals matters which should be well known. One should not gloss over a shining chapter in the fight for Irish freedom.

"I have heard children going to school being taunted by other children with remarks like, 'His father was a gunman. He shot people'—referring to the part played by their fathers in the war of independence. This veil of secrecy applies in particular to the red-letter day, Bloody Sunday.

"Very few people and hardly any of the younger generation

understand or appreciate the all-important necessity for the action by the I R A on that Sunday. Above all hardly anybody truly appreciates the authority which backed that action nor, indeed, the perfection of the action. How many appreciate that the course of Irish history might well have run differently if failure or cancellation had taken place? The action taken on Bloody Sunday by the I R A was taken under the only lawful governmental authority in Ireland. The I R A had been since the previous year the defence arm of the Irish Republican Government—acting under the authority of the Government which had been elected by the vast majority of the Irish people.

"It had duly given the Government its allegiance and its members had sworn to defend it in the following terms: 'I do solemnly swear (or affirm) that I do not, and shall not, yield a voluntary support to any pretended Government, Authority or Power inside Ireland hostile or inimical thereto; and I do further swear (or affirm) that to the best of my knowledge and ability I shall support and defend the Irish Republic, which is Dail Eireann, against all enemies foreign and domestic and that I will bear true faith and allegiance to the same and that I take this obligation freely without any mental reservation or purpose of evasion. So help me God.'

"The oath had been administered to my own Company at 34 Lower Camden Street in the early part of 1919. I was a section commander in that Company—'C' Company of the 3rd Battalion Dublin Brigade. The Company was under command of Captain Paddy Flanagan, a participant with the same unit in the 1916 rebellion. This Company distinguished itself in harassing the British troops, Auxiliaries and police in its area—particularly along the streets running from South Saint George's Street to Kelly's Corner—so much so that this area had earned itself the title of 'the Dardanelles'—after a notoriously dangerous area in World War I. I do not know if it was the British themselves who so christened it, but it may be stated in truth that it was their experiences in that area in Dublin which drove them to seek protection within caged lorries and to adopt the unchivalrous method of carrying Irish prisoners of war as hostages in their lorries—a practice which later extended to the whole country.

"Some time during the Friday of November 19th, 1920, I received an order from Captain Flanagan to meet him that night at 8 p.m. in Montague Lane off Harcourt Street. On arriving there I saw another of the Company's non-commissioned officers—Albert Rutherford—leaving after a discussion with the Captain. When I approached the skipper (his best known title) he informed me that a most important operation against the British had been planned for the following morning. He then proceeded to tell me that General Headquarters in conjunction with the Minister for Defence and the Dail Cabinet had decided that a mortal blow should be aimed at the British Intelligence system in Dublin. He said that the position was serious and that it was now a question of which side would strike the deadly blow first. He handed me a piece of paper and warned me that it was most important that I should keep it safe as it contained the names of the British Intelligence Officers who resided at certain addresses with the numbers of their rooms or flats and particulars of those, if any, who lived with them. The Captain ordered me to meet him again on the following Saturday evening at, I think, 6 p.m., saying that he would then go into final details regarding the operation. Meanwhile I was, on Saturday afternoon, to reconnoitre the area surrounding the premises and let him have my views as to the necessary outposts required and a plan for the safe retreat of those operating within the houses. We discussed the arms position and the quantity available at 60 Haddington Road. This house was my own (and other army men's) address for some time—with me there were Hugh Brady, Geoff Keating and Leo Duffy. The latter was assistant to Jimmy Doyle, the Company's Quartermaster. All of us were attached to the same unit and most of us were attached to the Irish Republican Brotherhood, as were Captain Flanagan and most of the rest of the Company. After leaving the Captain that night I went home to Haddington Road and later that night discovered that my colleagues were also aware of the operations intended for Sunday morning.

"Next day as usual I went to work at insurance offices at 30 College Green, having safely secreted the instructions and list of offices given me by Captain Flanagan, on the inside of my pants. Just before noon on that Saturday, Auxiliaries rushed up the stairs with their revolvers in their hands and held up the offices. All the men there were searched and asked their names. I was placed under arrest and ordered to get out and into the lorry. I had no option nor any chance of escape. The list for next day's operations was my great concern. How could I get rid of it safely?

"When all the Auxiliaries were back in the lorry it drove down Great Brunswick Street (now Pearse Street) to a tailoring establishment where another member of our Company was arrested and placed beside me. He was Eamon O'Neil, a good friend of mine. I gave him the cold shoulder and we pretended not to know each other. After having called at three other addresses where other members of the 'C' Company were arrested, we drove to Dublin Castle.

"We were placed in the Auxiliaries' guard-room which overlooked Exchange Court. It was a regular bedlam—indescrib-

F*

able with words—with mad men waving revolvers all over the
place and occasionally having a pot-shot at something on the
wall. If the aim was good a prisoner would be approached
and told: 'That was practice for your heart, Paddy, for when
we take you out the back later.'

"My list was now becoming a greater anxiety to me in
view of the fact that if it was discovered I certainly would go
'out the back' and furthermore my companions outside would
be in danger of walking into very serious traps next day. I
thought, 'Does success or failure tomorrow depend on me?'
and I tried to steel myself to ensure that failure would not
result. We had arrived at the Castle guard-room about 1 p.m.
and there were other prisoners there, none of whom I knew.
Up to 3 p.m. nothing worse had happened than the Auxiliaries' target practice and threats. A stout man arrived from
the cook-house with some cold swill which he said was tea
and slices of dry bread. He seemed to be the only human being
we had so far encountered in the Castle, for he said with a
sympathetic smile: 'I'm sorry lads. I can't do better.'

"This was the first time we prisoners had the opportunity
or excuse to move from the places we occupied sitting on
the old army beds. The swill and dry bread were placed on a
table near the window looking out into Dame Street through
Exchange Court. At this stage I had succeeded in removing
the incriminating document from where it had been pinned
inside my pants and now had it in my waistcoat pocket, where
it was procurable at quick notice. On moving from the old
bed to the table to eat my 'dinner' I turned to take my shoes
off the bed, and in doing so succeeded in putting the list of
British Intelligence officers into my mouth. It was the most
cherished meal I ever ate—even if a bit on the frugal side!
About the other worries I could do nothing for the moment.

If only I could get word to my colleagues outside that every-thing was all right—that the list was demolished and that I had not given my correct address, but one at which I had not resided for a considerable time.

"Sometime about 4 p.m. we had a visit from two Dublin Metropolitan Police detectives who examined us visually, asked our names and addresses, when and where we had been arrested, and so on. These two men were well known to me by sight and I knew one of their names. He was a man who Captain Flanagan had told me was friendly some time before when we met him in Camden Street. What the Captain said was: 'See that man on the inside, don't ever bother about him wherever you see him, he is friendly and that's for yourself and no one else.' He told me his name.

"Immediately I had seen the two detectives I recognized our friend and wondered if there was anything sinister in his approach to us. The two detectives turned and were walking away when our friend turned sharply back and asked: 'Had you fellows any grub since you came in here?' 'Yes, sir,' I answered, 'we had cold tea and some bread as dry as that'—holding a piece of newspaper up to him and putting it in my mouth to chew. 'We enjoyed it all the same,' I added. The detectives then left and I was not sure if our friend took the tip that the all-important piece of paper had met with the same fate as the bit of newspaper he saw going into my mouth. Certain after-events convinced me that he did and that he passed the information on to the proper quarter. Anyhow my pals did not leave our digs at 60 Haddington Road and no alteration was made in Sunday's plans, which went ahead as arranged.

"Shortly after the detectives left we were ordered by the Auxiliaries into a passage leading from the guard-room out into the Castle yard and thence into a lorry waiting outside. We were then confronted with a new departure, we were ordered to act as guides and to conduct them to our houses. What a blessing in disguise! I was the first to be arrested and apparently the first on the list. I told the driver to turn left outside the Castle gate, directed him up High Street, Thomas Street, Meath Street and into Reginald Street to No. 11, the address I had given but where I had not resided for a lengthy period. My ex-landlady, Mrs Flately, opened the door to my knock. She was amazed when she realized the position. I had succeeded, on entering the hallway, in tipping my lips with my index finger—a signal which she promptly understood. After the house was searched and nothing incriminating found we proceeded to New Street, the home of Eamon O'Neil. The search there was abortive also and after visiting the houses of the other prisoners we returned to Dublin Castle. It was now about 5 p.m. and the guard-room population had increased by the addition of other prisoners brought in since we left. A number of the prisoners were now brought separately to the Intelligence room for interrogation. Three Auxiliary officers were seated at a table, revolvers beside them—two others on each side of the prisoners. Questions started with the usual formal ones:

" 'What is your name? . . . 'Bryan Doyle.'

" 'How do you spell it? . . . 'B-r-y-a-n D-o-y-l-e.'

" 'Do you know Ben Doyle?' . . . 'No, sir.'

" 'Do you know Simon Donnelly?' . . . 'No, sir.'

" 'Do you know Paddy Flanagan?' . . . 'No, sir.'

" 'Didn't you meet Paddy Flanagan last night in Harcourt Street?'

" 'No, sir. You must be making a mistake.'

"At this stage the standing Auxiliaries had their revolvers

touching my cheeks and a lame-legged Auxiliary officer [Captain Hardy] said to him: 'Don't fire till I give you the order. Do you know Sean Guilfoyle?' . . . 'No, sir.'

" 'I'll order them to blow your bloody brains out. What's your address? . . . No. 11 Reginald Street.'

" 'We have been to that house, sir,' said one of the Auxiliaries beside me.

" 'Did you find anything?'

" 'No, sir.'

" 'Take him away—we'll deal with him later,' said the lame-legged officer.

"On returning to the guard-room I noticed that the number of prisoners had increased to twelve or fifteen. I thought how right Collins, G H Q and the Cabinet were in ordering a vital blow to be struck. The British Intelligence is gradually hounding us down. Flanagan—Donnelly—Guilfoyle, three of the most important officers in our Battalion! Did they know as much, or more, about other Battalions and other key-men?

"Before Sunday morning had passed, more startling events happened. During that night Liam Pilkington (alias Liam Scanlon) was brought in. Liam was a Commander of one of the Western Divisions of the I R A—had he been shadowed to Dublin?

"And then about 2 a.m. Brigadier Dick McKee and Vice-Brigadier Peadar Clancy were pushed in amongst us, and with them was Sean Fitzpatrick. What had gone wrong—what will happen tomorrow? Peadar gave me the same signal as I had given to my ex-landlady and I did not therefore make any move to recognize him, although I knew him well and had taken part with him in the disarming of the British garrison at the King's Inns. [This was one of the most daring and success-

ful daylight raids for arms by the I R A. A part of the I R A
which included the young Kevin Barry, strolled into the military barracks and within six minutes had held up the garrison
and escaped unscathed with twenty-five rifles, two Lewis
guns, several thousand rounds of ammunition and other military equipment. None of the soldiers was injured.]

"The early part of Sunday morning passed without incident
beyond the lengthy periods during which McKee and Clancy
were absent for interrogations. The remainder of the prisoners
were mostly light-hearted and gay, too much so in view of the
seriousness of their position. None of them knew of the events
which were happening in hotels and boarding houses that
morning. Amongst them was one quiet young man whom
nobody knew named Connor Clune.

"From noon to night of that Sunday the scene in that
Dublin Castle guard-room is beyond description—no words
of mine are adequate to picture it. The stark mad Auxiliaries
lost all traits of being human. Suffering from the effects of the
blow that had been struck against the Intelligence, combined
with the fact that they were drinking whisky or gin, they
simply could do nothing except shoot—shoot—shoot and
drink more whisky and gin. There was nobody in control but
somehow they were making plans for the coming tragedy.
Apparently they could not execute up to twenty prisoners out
of hand so they were setting the stage for something 'explain-
able'. Under such conditions—knowing no one, speaking to
no one—one could only think.

"I thought of Padraic Pearse. I rehearsed the story of his
last poem in my mind. I pictured the last farewell of his
mother at the gate of St Endas in Rathfarnham on the Easter
Monday morning of 1916. I thought of his mother's last
request: 'Pat, won't you write a little poem for me—some-

thing that would appear to be said by me about you,' and the son's reply— 'Yes mother, I will.'

"I thought of Pearse in the cold candle-lit cell in Kilmainham jail in the early morning hours before his execution— 'Oh, I nearly forgot, mother asked me to write a little poem for her—something that would appear to be said by her about me.' I rehearsed in my mind that last poem of Pearse:

" 'Dear Mary, thou didst see thy first-born son
　Go forth to die amid the scorn of men
　For whom he died;
　Receive my first-born son into thy arms,
　Who also has gone forth to die for men,
　And keep him by thee till I come to him;
　Dear Mary, I have shared thy sorrow
　And soon will share thy joy.'

"I thought again—was there ever so much faith and hope and love enshrined in so few words! Love—love under these circumstances! I thought of Kevin Barry—Kevin who had been three years younger than myself. I thought of the Manchester Martyrs. 'Whether on the scaffold high or on the battlefield we die . . .'

"During the night of November 21st the prisoners in the guard-room were ordered to parade in single file in the passage leading out into the Castle yard. We stood for a little while waiting for the order to move forward. McKee, Clune and Fitzpatrick were not called on to join us—they were left sitting on the old beds near the fireplace. It seemed ages since we were marshalled into that file, and we then got the command to move. Suddenly a voice from the dark passage in front was heard: 'Stop. Hold on there a minute!' I was second or third last in the file, the end of which was in the room where the three prisoners sat. Third in front of me in the file was

Peadar Clancy—just out into the darkness of the corridor. The man who gave the order now appeared with an electric torch in his hand—it was the lame-legged Auxiliary officer, Hardy. He scanned each face with his torch, at the same time asking the prisoner's name. When he asked Peadar, he replied, 'Clancy'. Hardy examined him minutely with the torch and then said, 'Get over there, you bastard,' pointing to where McKee, Clune and Fitzpatrick were sitting. Then he beckoned Fitzpatrick to take Clancy's place in the line. Clancy had nearly escaped!

"We in the file were then all marched into the Castle yard, loaded into lorries and driven through the streets to Beggar's Bush Barracks. In the guard-room—just inside the main gate—we were told later by the Auxiliaries that our three pals had 'attempted to escape' from the Castle and had been shot. We felt that they were dead anyway so we prayed aloud for them.

"After spending a few days in the guard-room at Beggar's Bush—during which sleep or rest was impossible—we were moved to a prisoner's compound at the right-hand corner of the barrack square. There was a wooden hut there surrounded by barbed wire entanglement. The population of prisoners continued to increase steadily. There were men from the North City—the 1st and 2nd Battalion areas—including the brothers Ross and Paddy Malion whose fine printing works had been wrecked by the Auxiliaries. Also there were Paddy Young, Tommy O'Keefe and a member of my own 'C' Company, Mick O'Hanlon.

"Just as in Dublin Castle and the Beggar's Bush guard-room, rest and sleep were almost impossible. The Auxiliaries at Beggar's Bush were on a par with, if not actually more savage than, their colleagues in the Castle. Every half hour or so, day and night, they harassed the prisoners—took them out of bed, threatened them, brought them to the interrogation room, fired shots over their heads, and ordered them to run back from the interrogation room as they fired shots after them. It was hell.

"In quieter moments I thought about my mother and father. She was far away, he had been brought to Dublin and imprisoned in Mountjoy jail because he refused to recognize the British authority in Ireland. He had refused to pay a mere 5s. dog licence to them. Ireland, young and old, had given allegiance to Dail Eirann. I thought too of my Cumann-na-mban intended wife, Kathleen. [Cumann-na-mban was the Sinn Fein organization for women.]

"The prisoners began to get organized and complained bitterly and frequently to the officer in charge of the Auxiliaries —Major Briggs. We were surprised to find out that our complaints were news to him. He listened to us attentively and assured us that he would deal with them in due course. The prisoners had nick-named him 'The Canary' because he wore a heavy woollen yellow pullover.

"One day we were surprised to see that our hut was guarded by a number of British soldiers and we learned from them that Portobello or Wellington military barracks had been phoned by 'The Canary' and requested to send a detachment of soldiers to mount guard over us. We learned too from the 'Tommies' that their orders from 'The Canary' were: 'Shoot anyone who approaches the prisoners' compound night or day without permission from me!'

"One morning about 2 a.m. we heard a shot outside our compound, and almost simultaneously we heard a soldier call out: 'Halt. Who goes there?' The reply was not audible. The further command was—in the Lancashire accent to which we were now accustomed: 'If you advance another inch—eighteen inches lower will be my target.' We learned later that some of the Auxiliaries from Dublin Castle had approached to 'interview' a prisoner.

"The features of those comprising the main Auxiliary garrison at Beggars Bush became strange to us and we learned that some change had taken place—but thank heaven 'The Canary' was still with us. Soon we learned that the Beggar's Bush Company of Auxiliaries had left and been sent to Cork where they had encountered the 'boys from the County Cork' under Tom Barry and had received several salutary lessons. They were not dealing with helpless prisoners down there.

"Liam Pilkington escaped—walked out, it seems, in the clothes of a lady who had visited him. Everything had gone well with us, protected as we were by the British soldiers from the Auxiliaries—what an anomaly! But then we heard that these soldiers had protested at being in a position where they were forced to fire on, and perhaps kill, their own countrymen. The soldiers were withdrawn and once more we were left at the mercy of the Auxiliary lunatics. They came one night after some ambush or shooting in the city and dragged one of the prisoners half-naked out of bed and took him to the morgue in Londonbridge Road. When he returned, blood, which had flowed freely from a wound they inflicted on the back of his neck, was a mass of hard ice down his back. It was a bitter frosty night. I had a visit arranged by my cousins—the Murphy girls —from Father Albert, O.F.M. Cap. That was a wonderful tonic and I treasured for some twenty-five years afterwards a religious medal he gave me on that occasion. I had it inscribed 'From Father Albert. Beggar's Bush 1920'. 'God grant that Kathleen does not ask for "Ben" if she comes to visit me,' I thought. She did not—she asked for a prisoner named Doyle and was told there was a man named Bryan Doyle, was it he whom she wanted? He was the man, of course. My simple alias still held good.

"All the prisoners were transferred to Arbour Hill detention barracks. Athough conditions there were atrocious there was a lot of comfort in being in military custody away from the mad 'Auxies'. At first we were seven or eight in one small cell and were allowed out for a short spell only once a day. Later many of the prisoners were sent by sea to a concentration camp at Ballykinlar in Co. Down and we were then two or three to a cell.

"The Governor was a tall man who wore a monocle and was consequently known to us simply as 'Monocle'. He was a fairly considerate man, open to receive complaints and I pestered him once, twice, even three times a day. My story was I was there through a case of mistaken identity, that it was a shame to keep me, and that he should put it to higher authority so that I might get out before Christmas.

"One day in the yard at exercise I said to Joe McGrath [one of whose horses has since won the Derby], 'I may get out—I am persuading 'Monocle' that I am the wrong man.' 'Keep at it. One man outside is worth two hundred of us in here,' Joe replied, and he added, 'Don't be seen talking to me.' I had known that Joe was an officer in our army as I had seen him as a sitting member of a court-martial before which I had given evidence, but I did not know his position.

"It was now very near Christmas and I kept up the pressure on 'Monocle' for release. He sent for me on the day after Christmas Day and told me I was free to leave, and I walked out. I had no tram fare so I walked to Kathleen's house at Inchicore where I received a royal welcome. She told me that one of her brothers had been arrested and two of them were 'on the run'.

"When I reported back to my Company I was told that Captain Flanagan had been promoted to the rank of Commandant and placed in charge of the Dublin City Active Service Unit—we very much regretted his leaving us. His transfer made an election of officers necessary and this was held in the Painters' Hall, Gloucester Street (now called Sean McDermott Street). At the election 'little Joe' O'Connor was elected Captain and I was elected 1st Lieutenant.

"Commandant Flanagan transferred a number of men from our Company to the A S U including the three Jims—Gibbons, Doyle and Browne—and Dick Sweetman amongst others. Our Company was remarkable in view of the number of men it gave to the A S U on one hand and the rest of the country on the other. Dan Crowley, Andy Cooney, Ger Davis, Mick O'Hanlon (from Armagh), Tom Lawless, Hugh Brady, Louis D'Arcy, Denis Hiney, Ned Kellegher and others obtained special commissions from G H Q to stir up different areas in the country or on some other special service. In spite of the large number of men 'lost' in this way the Company kept up its activities in the 'Dardanelles' under the command of Joe O'Connor, Albert Rutherford, Ben Carty, Joe Sheppard and others. There was no slackening off and 'C' Company 3rd Battalion continued to be a guiding star in the Dublin Brigade. Good Dublin men are the best in Ireland!

"I asked Commandant Flanagan at this time for a transfer to the A S U as I felt that my simple alias could easily break down. He said he would, but a couple of days later told me that I could not be transferred to the A S U, as Michael Collins wanted me for a special job. I had not gone back to the Insurance Office at College Green but had obtained an outdoor appointment from the Insurance Company instead—one that would take me to various parts of the country.

"I met Collins in a day or two and got my assignment. He struck me as direct and very firm with a likeable gruffness and above all an affability behind his smile and a soft Cork accent which wiped away any other first impressions. May God have mercy on his soul!

" 'You were great in the Castle,' he said to me on parting, and the 'Big Fella' shook my hand and I saluted him. The action against the British agents by the Irish Government on Bloody Sunday brought the fight for Irish freedom to a stage where it was almost at an end. Collins in his book *The Path to Freedom* wrote: 'In my opinion the truce of July 1921 could have been secured in December 1920 . . . but the opportunity was lost through the too precipitate action of certain of our public men and public bodies. . . . It was a struggle between two rival Governments, the one an Irish Government resting on the will of the people and the other an alien Government depending for its existence on military force, the one gathering more and more authority, the other steadily losing ground and growing ever more desperate and unscrupulous.'

"Looking back I often think—wasn't it grand to have lived with that privileged generation of Irishmen."

11

THE FOLLOWING DAY

BLOODY SUNDAY was a busy one for the official writers of communiqués at Dublin Castle. Press men were badgering them, so were high officials, and they were faced with a bewildering sequence of events which had to be given the right slant. The secret service was involved. What complicated matters even more, the dead men had also been serving British officers. "Gangs of murderous assassins" was an easy phrase and the first one that came to the official mind, but how to explain the shooting down of innocent men, women and children by the allegedly discipined forces of the Crown was a different matter. Then, of course, there was the further complication of trying to explain how three unarmed prisoners safe in the heart of Dublin Castle could arm themselves and try to escape, so that all three of them had to be butchered whilst none of their guards was injured.

They laboured at their task and used a certain amount of ingenuity, with the result that next morning most of the newspapers of the world carried headlines condemning the wave of terrorism in Dublin which consisted only of the shooting of unarmed officers in their beds. The Croke Park incident was hardly mentioned and a few lines referred to the death of three prisoners killed whilst trying to escape.

Dr McLysaght of the National Library in Dublin, who was attached to the I R A intelligence in Co. Clare during the war of independence, told me about his friend Con Clune, whom the Castle authorities had posthumously promoted to the rank of Lieutenant in the 1st Battalion of the Co. Clare I R A.

"My father owned a seed and plant nursery at Rahere in Co. Clare at that time," said Dr McLysaght, "and we advertised for a clerk. We had two replies, one from Con Clune, the other from a man now prominent in the Irish Parliament—we accepted Con. Con worked in the office and had no connection with the rebels at all, although he was deeply interested in the Irish language and its revival and was a member of the Gaelic League.

"I had a car at the time and was very anxious in case it was commandeered by the British and damaged, so I decided to put it in a garage in Dublin where it would be safe until the troubles blew over. I told Con what I was going to do and asked him if he would like to ride to Dublin with me—I said it would give us the opportunity of seeing the football game at Croke Park as well. Con agreed and we arrived in Dublin on Saturday morning.

"We stopped at different hotels. On the way up he mentioned that he would try to see Piaras Beaslai to have a chat with him about the Gaelic League. I had arranged to meet him on the Sunday afternoon at a place near the entrance to the football ground. I went there as arranged but he did not turn up, so I decided not to go either and went back to my hotel.

"Next morning I read all about the shootings in Dublin and began to get worried about Con. In the evening papers I read his name and that he had been killed trying to escape. I read that his body was in the mortuary so I went there and recognized him—I was allowed to remove the body to a church.

"With the help of some friends, I later removed the body

to a garage and asked an ex-British officer named Colonel Pearson to have a look at Con's body. He did and he carefully examined the wounds and said that it was quite ridiculous to suggest that he had received such wounds whilst trying to escape.

"The following day I was sent for by Michael Collins to whom I told the whole story, and he asked me to go to London to give a complete account of everything. In London I saw Lord Simon and Oswald Mosley, who was an M.P. at the time. I also went to see Mr Asquith. His clerk told me that Mr Asquith could not see me, so I told him that I would sit in the waiting-room until he did. I waited for hours in a most uncomfortable state because I badly wanted to go to the toilet, but I was afraid to leave the room in case they would not let me back. In the end he agreed to see me but it did not do a lot of good and as far as I can remember he told me to 'wait and see'.

"When I returned to Dublin I was arrested and, by a strange coincidence, lodged in the same place where they had killed the three men. Indeed one of the Auxiliaries pointed to bullet holes in the woodwork and said to me, 'That's where we shot the other bastards, and we will probably do the same to you.'

Piaras Beaslai remembered meeting Clune: "I arrived at Vaughan's Hotel to see Dick McKee, and Clune was there. He spoke to me in Irish. I must have met him before but I did not remember him. We soon established our identities. He was with Sean O'Connell, who had brought him to Vaughan's to meet me. I talked with him and then excused myself for a little while to go upstairs to talk to McKee—he was with Michael Collins and a few others. I asked if I could see him again next day but he said, 'Things may be difficult tomorrow.' I never saw him again. I went back to continue my chat with Clune. When the Tans arrived I slipped out the back, leaving poor Con, who had nothing whatever to fear as he had no connection with the movement."

The British *Morning Post* carried the following account of the Croke Park massacre:[1]

"BLOODSHED AT HURLING MATCH
FIRE OF REBELS RETURNED

"A message received in London late yesterday afternoon stated that the authorities had reason to believe that the Sinn Fein 'gunmen' went to Dublin under the pretence of attending a hurling match between Dublin and Tipperary, but really to carry out the morning's murders.

"A mixed force of Military and R I C, added the message, surrounded the ground at Crow [sic] Park where the match was to have been held yesterday afternoon. They were fired on by Sinn Fein pickets when they were seen approaching and they returned the fire killing and wounding a number. About 3,000 men were then searched and afterwards many revolvers were found on the ground. A woman and a man in addition to the casualties already mentioned were killed in the crush owing to the crowd stampeding."

The mistake of calling it a hurling instead of a football match nearly led to the death of the Viceroy of India in faraway Bombay.[2] There, a young Christian Brother—Christian Brothers are a religious teaching order—read that the goalkeeper of the Tipperary hurling team had been shot by the British forces. The hurling goal-keeper was his brother. The young Christian Brother forgot all his Christian charity and went straight away to the school laboratory. There he manufactured a large and dangerous bomb which he determined to hurl into the British Viceroy's carriage. Later information, however, corrected the previous message and stated that it was a football match, thus saving another bloody incident.

Even the British newspapers most sympathetic to the Irish cause were shocked by the shooting of the secret-service men. The official story stated that they were innocent, unarmed men, that many of them had been killed in the presence of their wives and even that some Irish women had taken part in the shootings.

Hugh Martin, of the *Daily News*, was one British journalist who had seen events for himself in Ireland and whose efforts were aimed at telling the British people the truth about the "police" work in Ireland. He spared nothing in describing the reign of terror which the forces of the Crown were vigorously and successfully prosecuting, and nothing in condemning the murders of innocent people. In Tralee, the Black and Tans tried to capture and shoot him. On one occasion he was stopped and questioned as to the whereabouts of the "bastard Martin". He put up with the insult but was not very helpful under the circumstances.

The events of that morning in Dublin did not altogether surprise him, he wrote the following day:[3] "The news from Dublin will surprise least those who have been most closely in touch with the Irish tragedy during the past few months. It is indeed the inevitable consequence of recent Government policy or lack of policy.

"Some weeks ago I was informed that the police plan was to make country districts so unhealthy for active Republicans that they would be forced into the cities—more particularly Dublin—where they could be run to earth and captured in a series of sweeping police and military drives.

"Concurrently with this gradual concentration in the

capital of the more violent of Nationalist opinion raids by troops, aided by the Auxiliary division of the R I C, have become increasingly numerous and stringent. They seem, however, to have been singularly ineffective. Comparatively few arrests have been made.

"At the same time the unnecessary terrorism with which the raids have been conducted has still further inflamed the minds of the population and added fuel to the fire amongst the refugees themselves.

"'Perhaps the most astonishing thing to those who have known in a general way, if not in detail, what has been happening below the surface of the national life is the temerity with which the policy of reprisals was pressed forward. Prominent Government officials, police officers and military men, with whom I have discussed the position at length, have seemed to have no conception of the intense bitterness and fanatical hostility of the people among whom they lived. While believing that no alternative existed to a scheme of ruthless repression only comparable with that followed by the Germans in Belgium and Northern France, they yet saw no reason for going 'the whole hog' and imposing a system of legalized frightfulness.

"Thus it happens that officers have been left at the mercy of a gang of desperadoes fighting with their backs to the wall to avoid capture, and determined as the pressure increased day by day to take as many lives as possible before sacrificing their own.

"It is not fashionable in Ireland at the present time to talk about the risks run by either side. For those who live in Ireland know that whatever is happening there is war however veiled by the forms of police duty or however distorted by indiscipline or savagery.

"The only surprising point is that the breaking-point was not reached weeks ago. The death in prison of the Lord Mayor of Cork hurt the heart of the country far more than is even yet realized on this side of the Irish Channel. It swung men and women over into the activist camp who twelve months ago could hardly have imagined themselves on speaking terms with any of its denizens.

"The fearful reprisals during the past three months—including a number of murders or unofficial 'executions' by the police closing with those at Cork a few days ago—formed a dark setting for this national grief. The threat to starve Ireland into submission by shutting down her railways and prohibiting motor traffic added some still darker touches.

"But in my view the execution by hanging of young Kevin Barry, the seventeen-year-old medical student, who was implicated in the shooting of a soldier in Dublin did more than any other single incident to precipitate the present crisis.

"I am speaking with close knowledge of the facts that that act of cold 'justice' was contrary to the wishes of the Prime Minister and of the Chief Secretary, that it was not approved by any member of the Irish Executive and had the active support neither of Sir Nevil Macready nor of Lord French.

"It was forced upon the Government fom another quarter with the threatened resignation of a very high and peculiarly influential official if Barry was reprieved.

"I state these facts not to palliate the crime of the assassins but to explain." The influential official referred to by Hugh Martin was Sir Henry Wilson.

The London *Times* wrote:[4] "Gangs of assassins in circumstances of revolting brutality murdered at least 14 British officers and ex-officers and wounded five more. . . .

"The leaders of Sinn Fein see now the harvest of their own

wicked folly, blinded by self conceit, disdainful of the British people, whose history and whose character they have alike ignored, they have not been averse from turning to their own political account, the murders which a criminal organization amongst their fellow countrymen have perpetuated. . . .

"In so far as the power of the Government can produce the arrest and punishment of the criminals it must be exercised to the full. It is however in circumstances such as these that justice most needs to be above reproach. We do not believe that in normal circumstances these murders could meet with aught but reprobation from the mass of the Irish nation. But an army already perilously indisciplined and a police force avowedly beyond control, have defiled by heinous acts the reputation of England while the Government who are trustees of that reputation are not free from suspicion of dishonourable connivance."

The *Times* a few days afterwards:[5] "Death was intended for many other officers than those actually killed and stories of wonderful escapes are common today. In one case an officer whose house was entered was in his bath but was able to escape through a back window. He owes his life to the courage and presence of mind of his wife who kept the raiders in talk whilst he escaped. In another case the house of a distinguished officer was searched from top to bottom but he had spent the night in another part of the city.

"I learn that the plan of attack was arranged some time ago and was reserved for an emergency which was held to have arisen when the Military Intelligence got hotly on the trail of the chief conspirators.

"No section of the Irish press conveys its horror at the murders or its despair at the social or political outlook, but the Nationalist papers hold strongly that the reprisals are largely responsible for the state of complete chaos into which the country is drifting. They denounce the shootings in Croke Park in which 10 or 12 people lost their lives."

The *Daily News* commented:[6] "Who can doubt that it will be followed in the course of the next few days by a renewed outbreak of violent reprisals which for the most part will fall as usual on innocent people. . . ? And murder will continue first on one side, then on the other, just as long as the British Government chooses to perpetuate in its odious and hopeless scheme of blind pitiless indiscriminate revenge."

The *Manchester Guardian* explained the events like this.[7] "The work of the assassin this morning is unquestionably a dreadful act of re-assertion by desperate men, who are feeling the pressure of an increasingly efficient intelligence service. It has been obvious to anyone watching the trend of affairs that the net has been drawn closer about the men and that their freedom of movement has been becoming every day more circumscribed.

"Six or nine months ago the authorities were without an intelligence service of any account and were seeking to cope with murder and conspiracy under the direction of an amazingly well informed intelligence department.

"Today the revolutionaries are confronted with an intelligence service recruited from some of the best brains employed in army intelligence work during the war. For weeks past now there have been daily raids in the city frequently on an extensive scale. . . .

"This morning's murders seem to have been directed at persons in the Army's legal and secret intelligence activities. Several of the dead officers were engaged either upon impending courts-martial or in preparing evidence for them and others belonged to the intelligence services."

The *Morning Post*, a rabid Unionist paper, commented:[8] 'Sinn Fein crime, cold blooded and brutal as it has been since the 'war' was declared on the British Government, reached its apogee so far in the campaign in what may be described as a massacre of British military officers and ex-officers residing out of barracks in various parts of the Irish capital. The attacks were obviously organized, cleverly planned and ruthlessly carried out.

". . . It appears that about 9 a.m. the houses of the men were visited by civilians who came in most cases accompanied by women guides."

An official report issued by Dublin Castle later read: "In one way or another ten officers who were killed were connected with the administration of justice, the collection of evidence and the prosecution of persons before courts-martial. It would seem that the Sinn Feiners were becoming alarmed at the quantity of information which the authorities were receiving, and they decided to destroy the evidence and, at the same time, terrorize the officers connected with the machinery of justice."

In this connection a conversation I had with an ex-I R A officer, Liam O'Breen from Galway, is worth noting. "Shortly after Bloody Sunday I was captured by the British in the West of Ireland," he told me, "and was questioned by one of their intelligence men. I was very scared indeed as I knew what to expect. During the examination, however, it became clear to me that he was nervous too, so I took a grip on myself and talked myself out of detention. As I walked away I said to myself, 'Thanks be to God, Mick. You've put the the wind up them properly with your Bloody Sunday.' "

A couple of days after Bloody Sunday, a crowded House of Commons listened to a long statement on the events of that awful day by Sir Hamar Greenwood, Under-Secretary of State for Ireland. The house was hushed and shocked by the terrible catalogue of executions. Sir Hamar spared no efforts to impress upon his listeners the horror of that morning. He referred to "the cruel and savage massacre and wounding of unarmed British officers". There were loud cheers when he said that four of the assassins had been captured red-handed with guns, and when the cheering died down an Irish M.P. shouted, "Are they still alive?" He said that Cadets Garnin and Morris were the first two casualties suffered by the Auxiliaries "who were doing such splendid work in Ireland". At the Gresham Hotel, he told his horrified audience, who shouted out "shame", one of the assassins had finished off one of the officers with a sledge-hammer.

When Joe Devlin, a member of the Irish Nationalist Party which still sat in Parliament in those days, arose to ask a question there were cries of "sit down" from all parts of the House.

Sir W. Davison was allowed to speak and he asked the Prime Minister if he was aware that Parliament at one sitting would give him whatever power would be necessary to stamp out the active murder campaign and grant immediate legislation to shoot anybody carrying arms or ammunition in any disturbed area in Ireland? [9]

The Prime Minister explained that he had enough power already: "We are convinced that the Irish Authorities are gradually succeeding in their gallant efforts to break up the gang of assassins who have been terrorizing Ireland." By "Irish Authorities" he meant the British Authorities in Ireland.

Indeed the Prime Minister had his own ideas about the murdered officers and told an Irish businessman, Mr Moylett, a few weeks afterwards: "They got what they deserved. Beaten

Radio Times Hulton Picture Library

A familiar street scene in the Dublin of 1920: Auxiliaries with drawn revolvers search a Post Office van.

Radio Times Hulton Picture Library

The funeral of two British Intelligence officers in Dublin, 24 November 1920. Auxiliaries carry the wreaths and Black and Tans line the route.

Ben Doyle

Ben Doyle and his Cumann-na-mban wife, Kathleen, whose services to the Irish cause included frequent trips to England to help smuggle arms to the IRA.

(Right) March 1921: Paddy Moran and Thomas Whelan in Mountjoy Prison the evening before they were hanged. Between them is the Black and Tan who offered to effect Moran's escape.

National Museum of Ireland

by counter-jumpers." "Counter-jumpers" being a rather derogatory description of a young man who works in a store or shop.

Mr Joe Devlin continued his attempts to ask a question, in spite of continued shouts of "sit down", and eventually the Speaker let him have his say.[10]

"I wish to ask," he said, "why, when questions are asked as to these horrible occurrences nothing is said about the appearance of military forces on a football field."

Indignant members shouted louder, "Sit down . . . sit down." The members were really roused now by this damned Irishman who wanted to bring up such a ridiculous incident.

"I will not sit," he yelled and tempers now reached fever pitch. Members near Devlin stood up, shouting at him, and suddenly Major Molson, normally a mild and inoffensive man, threw his arm around Devlin's neck and tried to drag him back to his seat. Other members intervened and a general scrimmage developed whilst the Speaker called hopelessly for order. Mr Jack Jones and Mr Hoggs tried to separate the contestants, but now from all sides of the house the infuriated British M.P.s shouted: "Kill him. . . . Kill him."

The scrimmage continued and Devlin shouted: "Is this English courage—attacking one man in six hundred?" Finally Mr Jones forced himself between the two M.P.s and Mr Hoggs and Mr T. P. O'Connor held Mr Devlin. Pale and dishevelled, he struggled to free himself and eventually did break away. Then he swung a tremendous swipe at Major Molson—at that critical moment another M.P., a Mr Higham, stepped forward and received the full force of the blow in the face; his face was bruised and his lip cut.

Another Irish M.P. whose name is lost to posterity cried exultantly: "There's reprisals for you."

G

The voice of the Speaker was now heard and he suspended the sitting. Mr Lloyd George was an interested spectator of the fight, and he now turned and discussed it with his near neighbours, Mr Bonar Law and Sir Hamar Greenwood. Mr Winston Churchill was another fascinated spectator and he gave a spirited account of the encounter to an M.P. who had just arrived, enthusiastically swinging his fists to show how it had developed. Winston also had his own ideas about the British officers and told Sir Henry Wilson that "they were careless fellows who ought to have taken precautions".

Fifteen minutes later the sitting was resumed after Major Molson had apologized to Mr Devlin and Mr Devlin had apologized to Mr Higham.

THE DAY THE LIFFEY RAN BLACK WITH HATS

O n Thursday November 26th, nine bodies of the secret service men passed through Dublin on their way to a Royal Naval destroyer which was tied up at North Wall, a quay near the heart of the city. The nine bodies returning to England for burial were those of Major Dowling, Captain Newbury, Captain Bagally, Captain Price, Lieutenant Bennett, Lieutenant Ames, Lieutenant McMahon and the Auxiliaries Garnin and Morris.

Describing the funeral the Dublin correspondent of the *Daily Telegraph* wrote:[1] "Dublin saw the most expressive funeral demonstration that has taken place within the memory of living citizens. . . . As a token of respect and fitting reverence to men whom all regard as martyrs to the sacred principle of duty every business house within the city closed its doors and there was a suspension of business between 10 a.m. and 1 p.m. . . . the few among them who by seeking to keep open their establishments had thought to offer insult to the dead were brought to reason if not to mood for reverence. Early in the day Auxiliary Police went to such establishments and ordered those—who owned or managed them—to close. The order was sufficient.

The general attitude of those who formed this vast assemblage was the attitude of reverence but among them on the quays were some who had been prompted by that last and meanest of all human motives—the desire to slight the honourable and the honoured dead. These sections whilst the great majority of spectators stood with bared heads kept their heads still covered as the funeral approached. Amongst them there were also those who smiled and sought to create ill-timed merriment. Auxiliary police appeared and ordered them to take off their hats and cease smiling. At first these ill-bred demontrators were unwilling to obey. Then came the order in a quiet but compelling voice: 'Stop laughing or get behind'—behind was nothing but the river. 'Take off those hats or we will shoot them off,' said another quiet voice. The hats came off and those who removed them hesitated to replace them even when the funeral was past. Others who scattered through the crowd and persisted in remaining with head covered had their hats thrown into the Liffey by young men in their immediate neighbourhood and were invited to go in after them. . . .

"Upwards to a thousand troops took part in the procession, aeroplanes flew overhead and an armoured car led whilst a second followed the procession."

From another source we learn that more than hats were thrown into the unpleasant waters of the river Liffey. The *Daily Express* correspondent, with a touch of humour, wrote that as well as hundreds of hats flowing majestically towards the open sea were many young men who had "mysteriously" been cast into the waters.[2] A young and fascinated spectator of the floating hats was Gerald Tickell, author of *Odette* and several other excellent books, who told me: "The river was black with hats of every size and colour and shape—it was a most astonishing sight." Early on Bloody Sunday morning the young Gerry had stared at another strange sight—part of the body of the unfortunate Captain Newbury as it hung out of a window in Lower Baggot Street.

There was another long but much quieter funeral in Dublin. It was that of the victims of the Croke Park "affray". But the Crown forces had forbidden anybody but the nearest relatives to accompany them to their graves.

Accompanying the dead officers on the destroyer were parties of the R I C and Black and Tans and members of the Auxiliaries who were to march in the funeral procession in London. The R I C band were also on board.[3] One of the musicians accidentally dropped his cornet in its case overboard. The destroyer reversed whilst sailors fished it out from amongst the floating hats.

At 9.30 a.m. the following morning a magnificent and impressive funeral cortège left Euston station in London and marched through silent crowds to Westminster, where six of the bodies were taken into Westminster Abbey for the Requiem service whilst the bodies of the three Catholic officers, Bennett, Ames and McMahon went to Westminster Cathedral for Requiem Mass.

The procession was led by the massed bands of the Brigade of Guards and Household Cavalry—pipers, drummers and buglers. The coffins were on gun carriages, and the procession included detachments of men from the Metropolitan Police, the City Police, the Fire Brigade and the Salvage Corps. At the Abbey there were a hundred members of the House of Commons including the Prime Minister, Mr Lloyd George and Mr Winston Churchill, and a hundred members of the House of Lords. At Westminster Cathedral the King was represented by General the Earl of Cavan; with him were Mr Bonar Law and Mr Austen Chamberlain. The band of the Royal Irish Constabulary played outside the cathedral.

After the service the coffins went their several ways in the charge of relatives. Cadet Morris was buried at Bandon Hill

Cemetery, Croydon, and amongst the many wreaths was one from the Mayor and Corporation of Croydon.

Describing the procession in London, the *Evening News* reporter wrote:[4] ". . . and I wonder again if one of the guilty men is amongst that scattering crowd with the blood reeking on his hands and the stench of foul murder rising from his heart; I wonder if this man trembles and grows faint as he knows secretly that the furies, the dark maidens with serpents twining in their hair and the black blood dripping from their eyes, are following him and hunting him, hounding him on to an awful and bloody end."

The "guilty" men were too concerned at that juncture with the human furies who were hounding them to worry about the ghostly ones.

The Auxiliaries continued their sudden violent swoops on houses or areas in the city in the hope of catching armed members of the I R A. Usually, however, the moment a member of the I R A saw that he was in danger of being searched he dropped his firearm or hid it. On one occasion as a Dublin painter was on a ladder decorating the ceiling of a house in the city, an I R A man ran into the room and said: "The Tans are surrounding the house. Where can I hide my revolver?" The painter reached down and, taking it from him, put it into the long large pocket in the front of his overall, covering it with a few paint brushes. When the Black and Tans entered the room the painter walked through them carrying a pot of paint. He walked down the street to a safe pub, where he found another I R A man. "Would you like to buy a good ·45 revolver?" said the painter. "I would, of course," said the I R A and paid over 45s. for it. "A bob for every point—sure 'twas very fair," the painter told me.

Next day, however, the same painter was in the same room

getting on with the ceiling when the first I R A walked in and asked for his revolver. "I gave it to one of your fellows for forty-five bob," said the painter unhesitatingly. His hearer was shocked. "I'll have to report you to the officer in charge," he told the painter and straight away went off for the officer. He listened to the whole story and then philosophically remarked, "I suppose it's fair enough—we'll have to look upon the forty-five shillings as a cloak-room fee," and he thanked the painter for saving a sorely needed weapon and possibly a man as well.

The painter's son told me of another occasion during a sudden swoop by the Auxiliaries when he was but a very small baby in a cot. "It seems—my mother told me—that the Auxis rushed in suddenly and began to search the room. I would not stop crying and one of them patted me on the head—but my mother swore at him and pushed him away. Indeed I had every right to cry—I was lying on two very knobbly revolvers which had just been pushed underneath me. Sure," added Bill Kavanagh, " 'tis marvellous what I put up with for auld Ireland!"

The *Spectator*, a stout and influential Unionist weekly paper, was a most bitter critic of the I R A, whom it usually described as "murderers" or "assassins". It buried its head deeply in the sands of British Imperialism and vehemently condemned the Irish for wishing to be rid of the forces which for hundreds of years had tyrannized and looted the country. Looking back now it seems quite fantastic that groups of respectable British people fanatically urged the Government to suppress with any kind of ferocity the will of the Irish people as expressed in a well-conducted and democratic General Election. These groups supported the policy of unofficial reprisals which made life a frightful hell for the men, women and children living in their own country and had little or no effect upon the Irish Republican Army.

Commenting on Bloody Sunday the *Spectator* wrote:[5] "We are bound to say that the callousness with which the Irish Nationalist press and the National members in the House of Commons sought to divert attention from the 'killings' of the officers by exaggerating and distorting an affray at Croke Park seems to us almost as horrible as the murders themselves."

Any neutral referee would agree that the British won easily on points in frightfulness on that Sunday. The "affray" in question cost twelve civilian lives and sixty injured compared with the deaths of secret service men in the morning who, courageous as they undoubtedly were, knew the risks they were taking in challenging the secret army of the other side.

The *Spectator* went on: "The massacre of Sunday morning was the direct outcome of the tolerance, nay the levity with which for the last year we as a Nation have treated the rising tide of murder in Ireland."

About the same time Mr Asquith, ex-Prime Minister of England, had described the shooting of an Irish mother, Mrs Quinn, by British forces as wilful murder. This coincided with the shooting of an R I C Sergeant named James O'Donoghue by the I R A in Cork city. The *Spectator* differentiated between the deaths like this:[6] "Mrs Quinn was killed through the reckless and culpable discharge of firearms by a lorry load of constables maddened by the thought of death in ambush for them in any corner, and by remembrance of comrades cruelly done to death in cold blood. Now the case of the R I C Sergeant shot dead is a real case of wilful murder. To confuse it with a case such as that of Mrs Quinn is to debase the moral currency."

The bitterness with which the *Spectator* and its sober body of supporters felt towards the Irish fight for independence is illustrated by the following excerpts:[7]

"Numerous assassinations are reported from Ireland; most of these appear to be attributable to quarrels within the Sinn Fein ranks or to fear of informers which brings every Irish conspiracy to an end."

On the burning of Cork by the Auxiliaries:[8] "All we want to do now is to protest against the assumption that there is something inherently improbable in Irishmen burning their own buildings. On the contrary all past experiences suggest that this is just the kind of thing they would be capable of doing." Such reports must have infuriated "K" Company of the Auxiliaries who were proud of their efforts.

With reference to this same company of Auxiliaries the *Spectator* wrote:[9] 'A tragic incident of last week was the shooting of Canon Magner by a cadet in a fit of insanity. The unhappy officer was one of the few survivors of the terrible outrage at Kilmichael near Macroom in which his comrades were brutally done to death and the shock had unhinged his mind." There were, as we have seen, no survivors from the Kilmichael ambush.

The name "Bloody Sunday" in Ireland generally means only the massacre at Croke Park. The senseless slaughter at the football match is remembered more than the immediate reason for it. The British people at that time believed that chivalrous unarmed British Officers had been foully murdered and most of them ignored the Croke Park incident. The Irish people forgot about the shootings of the British murder gang and built up the bloody reprisal as an event of national importance. The fact is that the shootings of the morning constituted the most vital action in the whole history of the Irish war of independence.

The conviction in British Government circles that the I R A was composed of lawless gangs of murderers led by louts from the bogs of Ireland was shattered. The intelligence officers who had been recruited for the Irish "job" included many of the most experienced and most courageous in the British Army. The British leaders accepted the fact that this ruthless and well-organized action had destroyed their intelligence system in Ireland, and with that gone they had but stark force left to solve their Irish problem.

Within a few weeks the British Government had put out feelers for a truce. Feelers that were withdrawn when the I R A refused to lay down their arms to achieve it. But the offer had been made, an offer that was subsequently repeated at frequent intervals until eventually it led to the "cease fire" on 11 July, 1921, with the I R A keeping their arms. That was not to be for many months, however, and in the meantime the executions of the officers and the two Auxiliaries whipped up the tempers of armed forces to greater frenzies.

The British intelligence force which had existed before Bloody Sunday did not normally report to or through the Dublin Castle authorities. They had realized that the I R A agents in the Castle revealed all its secrets to Collins, so the newly recruited force reported directly to London, but even that did not save them. The danger that had threatened the I R A Cabinet had been a very real and close one. If that danger had not been eliminated on Bloody Sunday morning the probability is that the Sinn Fein movement would have been wrecked.

Referring to it afterwards, Collins wrote:[10] "My one intention was the destruction of the undesirables who continued to make miserable the lives of ordinary decent citizens. I had proof enough to assure myself of the atrocities which this gang of spies and informers committed. Perjury and torture are words too easily known to them. If I had a second motive it was no more than a feeling such as I would have for a dangerous reptile.

"By their destruction the very air is made sweeter. That should be the future judgment on this particular event. For myself my conscience is clear. There is no crime in detecting and destroying, in war time, the spy and the informer. They have destroyed without trial. I have paid them back in their own coin."

On Bloody Sunday evening, as the lifeless bodies of British and Irish soldiers and of the men, women and children lay in morgues in the city, the Black and Tans and the military patrolled the streets in lorries and on foot with hate in their hearts. Curfew was supposed to begin at midnight but that night the Crown forces roamed the streets at seven o'clock, shouting to the people: "Go home, you bastards." Near Clare Street the Auxiliaries crashed their rifle butts into the faces of three men they held up and, when one of them ran away in his terror, shot him with grim deliberation.

The forces of the Crown became more dangerous now because they had become more scared. It is a nerve-racking experience to move about in a city fighting an enemy you cannot see, where every civilian is a potential gunman, and every corner and window a possible ambush position. It was bad enough before, but now the unseen forces of the I R A had proved their organization and their ruthlessness. There is usually a hope in every soldier's heart that their own intelligence service is all-powerful and all-knowing, but the "shinners" had even exposed the secret service and blasted it.

The I R A were not perturbed by the sensation they had caused.

Frank Teeling had been shot in the leg and captured by the Auxiliaries in a lane behind Upper Pembroke Street. He was the only I R A man taken that morning and he was, indeed, a most important capture because if he could be prevailed upon to speak, others could be taken into custody and charged. But Frank did not break under the most severe and roughly conducted interrogations. As soon as his wound had healed enough he was court-martialled, sentenced to death and sent to Kilmainham jail to await hanging.

Two other men were arrested and charged with complicity in the shootings. There was no direct evidence but some was manufactured and both of them, Paddy Moran and Tom Whelan, were sentenced to be hanged. They were lodged with Ernie O'Malley who too had been sent to Kilmainham after being tortured in Dublin Castle. O'Malley was one of the most determined, efficient and successful of the I R A leaders. A most methodical and cool-headed guerilla fighter, he had worked day and night to build up the I R A forces throughout the Midlands and South of Ireland. Now in British hands he was masquerading as "Bernard Stewart".

These men won the affection of the British soldiers who were saving them for the gallows. One of the guards provided O'Malley with strong wire-cutters and a ·38 revolver and the soldier offered to fight with them if their escape was contested.[11] Teeling was a special favourite of his captors—he was little more than a boy, a light-hearted and gay one who did not seem a bit disturbed by the fate which awaited him.

I R A outside the jail were alerted about the coming attempt at escape and they arrived at the lane adjoining the prison to discover that it was a favourite courting place for the military garrison. Several couples of lovers were rounded up at pistol point and placed in a nearby shed. The first attempt at

escape proved abortive because the prisoners did not know
how to use the wire-cutters correctly, so the lovers had to be
detained and fed with hot cocoa for a day and a night. The
soldier helped Teeling to use the cutters correctly and the
following night O'Malley, Teeling and a prisoner who had
just arrived at Kilmainham named Simon Donnelly walked
out. They told Paddy Moran about their escape and asked him
to come with them. Paddy, who was innocent of complicity
with the events of Bloody Sunday morning, refused. He could
not see how he could possibly be convicted and he did not
want to let his witnesses down. He should, of course, have
known better—all the inventors of evidence and believers in
perjury had not been killed on that Sunday morning, so Paddy
paid with his life for his faith in British justice.

Paddy Moran and Tom Whelan were hanged the following
March on the same morning as four other young men who
had been convicted of "high treason and levying war". The
night before the hangings Mr Ellis, the hangman from England, and three assistants arrived at the jail in a tank. At dawn
thousands of Dubliners knelt about the prison walls and prayed
for the men who were about to die. The scene was lit by the
light of blessed candles illuminating pictures of the Blessed
Virgin which were pinned to the granite walls. Mingling with
the crowd were tin-hatted and heavily armed soldiers who, it
was reported, were subdued, puzzled and sympathetic.

Inside the fortress everything was going smoothly, decor-
ously, and callously. The first pair of condemned men attended
mass and received communion together. Whelan served mass
and at 6 a.m. precisely Mr Ellis efficiently carried out the
sentence pronounced by the British court martial on the first
two men.

Mr Ellis and his assistants relaxed until 7 a.m. when they

carried out a similar operation on the next two men; at 8 a.m. the last two men were executed. Then after a decent interval Mr Ellis and his assistants climbed back into the tank and were borne safely through the streets of Dublin on their way back home to England.

The executions of these six men was yet another severe shock to the almost punch-drunk Irish people. Britain was acting true to type and the more cynical of the Irish were asking why the Governor had troubled to send Mr Ellis and his three assistants on the long dreary journey to Dublin when the whole of Ireland was hampered up with Auxiliaries and Black and Tans who would be glad of the job—if only for the kick of it!

Mr Lloyd George and his Government had been impressed by the events of Bloody Sunday and were even then searching for a way of negotiating with the leaders of the I R A, so the executions of these six men seem, in restrospect, quite senseless.

They were not the first, nor the last, to be killed because they were fighting for an independent Ireland, nor did they die in vain. The propaganda department of the I R A used this ammunition with good effect. The chief architect of the excellent information services of the I R A was the Englishman Erskine Childers—a man who never ceased to love England and the English people in spite of his allegiance to Sinn Fein. It was Childers, more than anybody else, who had ensured that the mass of the English people were informed of the crimes committed in their name against the people of Ireland. In the end it was the weight of decent English opinion, as expressed by influential and honest newspapers and by prominent and humanitarian figures in the English political scene, that forced the thoroughly dishonest Cabinet to come to terms and call an end to that last revolting chapter in Anglo-Irish history. The *Daily News* wrote:[12] "Certainly there are criminals in Ireland; if this [Croke Park] account be true there are criminal lunatics in England too and some of them are in charge of the Government."

Even in this day and age the British are woefully ignorant about Ireland and its people. Forty years ago this ignorance was even more widespread. To understand this one must live with the English people. I have heard an English mother telling a friend that her son in the Army had been sent to Belfast, and the other woman asked if that was in India or Egypt. The mother did not know but she laughed when her friend said, "I hope he won't bring back one of these black women with him." An intelligent Englishwoman asked me once: "I've heard a lot about the Black and Tan war in Ireland but I've never heard who won—was it the Blacks or the Tans?"

Even the very troops who served in Ireland came away in several cases without the slightest knowledge of what all the trouble was about. In the course of collecting material for this book I called upon an elderly Englishman in London who I was told had been a Black and Tan. In his shirt-sleeves, as he rolled himself a cigarette, he told me: "No, Guv. I was in Dublin all right, but I was the Royal Army Service Corps—driving chaps about and all that. There used to be a bit of shooting now and then but I never knew what it was all really about." I asked him if he had ever got into trouble there and he replied: "Never, mate. No, that's a lie—we did once. Me mates and me went into a pub for a drink and the fellow behind the bar points at a bunch of chaps at the end of the counter and tells us to clear out. We didn't argue, mate, we cleared out and went to a pub across the road."

It was ignorance such as this that Childers overcame by

dogged and skilful means. Michael Collins's genius would have been lost without the brilliant propaganda backing that Childers gave it. An Englishman himself, he knew the English mind better than any of the other leaders and, because of his work such statements as these appeared in the English press: "The treatment now being meted out to the Irish is nothing more nor less than indiscriminate vengeance"—the Rt. Rev. Dr Gore, Bishop of Oxford. "There is a tendency to hesitate in regard to the impeachment of the Government . . . whatever may have happened to the Government it is the duty of free Churchmen to protest against the policy which is at once, illegal, unjust, ineffective, and must be disastrous to Ireland and this country"—The Rev. Dr Clifford, leader of the Nonconformist Church.[13] "I say deliberately that never in the lifetime of the oldest amongst us has Britain sunk so low in the moral scale of Nations . . . things are being done in Ireland which would disgrace the blackest annals of the lowest despotism in Europe"—Lord Oxford and Asquith in a speech at London. "To give rein to lawlessness and allow indiscriminate forces to take matters into their own hands, to shoot at sight, to burn buildings, to reduce the whole system of the Governement to chaos is the worst application of force that can be imagined. The conscience of this country will not stand it and if it does the conscience of the civilized world will rise up in judgment against us"—The Rev. J. Scott Lidgett of the National Council of Evangelical Free Churches at Manchester on 10 March, 1921.

A British Labour Commission reported 28 December, 1920, that "in every part of Ireland we visited we were impressed by the atmosphere of terrorism that prevailed. We have no desire to overstate the facts but the atmosphere of terrorism which has been created and the provocative behaviour of the armed servants of the Crown quite apart from specific 'reprisals' are sufficient in themselves to arouse in our hearts feelings of the deepest horror and shame."

And the London *Times* wrote:[14] "Deeds have unquestionably been done by the forces of the Crown which have lastingly disgraced the name of Britain in that country. British processes of justice which for centuries have commanded the admiration of the world have been supplanted by those of 'lynch' law."

THE SIMPLE ANSWER

W A S Michael Collins justified in arranging and ordering the shootings of the British officers on Bloody Sunday morning? The extent and the results shocked even some of his own colleagues. Arthur Griffith, Acting President of Sinn Fein, was horrified—"In front of their wives on a Sunday in their own homes!" he said.

The simple answer is that Collins had no alternative if the fight was to be won. The men who were shot constituted a grave menace to the plans of the I R A. The battle was on. The British did not shrink from any method likely to be effective in crushing the guerilla army. When the war had started back in 1916 in the Dublin rebellion, the people of Ireland had condemned the I R A. But by 1920 the Irish people had seen the forces of Britain at work and were not only behind the I R A but were urging them to greater effort. Many who had been pro-British and whose sons—over 200,000 of them— had fought with the British Army against the Germans, had changed their views. In return for their sons' sacrifices at Mons, Ypres and every other battlefield during World War I, the British Government had unleashed undisciplined and cruel forces who treated the Irish as the Germans—they had been told—had treated the Belgians. Many of these soldiers were as sincere as the old Irish leader John Redmond, who wrote in 1916 about the Irish in the British Army:[1] "We see that our Irish troops in this war are fulfilling a mission. As

I said at the outset it is into their keeping, with the eyes of the World upon them, that the cause of their country for the time being has passed. The influence of their action upon her fortunes will extend far beyond the immediate effects which will appear the moment the war is over."

And the moment that war was over, Britain's demobilized soldiers were mobilized again to terrorize Ireland. The Irish people had seen this and had felt in their own homes and on their own bodies the "gratitude" of the British Government. Ireland was behind Collins, it had given his party a mandate and Collins had no alternative nor any wish to do anything but prosecute the war to its logical conclusion, which was to force Britain to grant the Irish independence.

Historically, the British had re-started the shooting war in Ireland—on 26 July, 1914, when the "King's Own Scottish Murderers" killed two men and a woman and injured thirty-two other people by firing on a crowd in Dublin. Historically, too, the British started the practice of shooting men in bed and in front of their wives and families. The charges of the Government spokesmen who condemned in horrified tones the executions of Bloody Sunday morning, ring hollow and hypocritical when one remembers the cold-blooded murder of fifteen-year-old Gleeson of Tipperary, for example, or of seventy-three-year-old Canon Magner in Cork. Neither is it true to say that the British excesses in Ireland were due to the insubordination of a few individuals under the influence, perhaps, of drink or shattered nerves. The Prime Minister himself was sure that the Sinn Feiners were being murdered by his own forces; Sir Henry Wilson, the Chief of Staff, advocated shooting by roster without trial or evidence; Sir Ormonde Winter, the British Chief of Intelligence, chortled over the killing of suspects "attempting to escape"; the Auxiliaries wore burnt corks in their hats, and even the military who claimed a good measure of discipline burned Mallow, looted Fermoy and blew up the houses of civilians as "unofficial reprisals".

In the face of such behaviour by the occupying forces of the Crown, was Collins justified in approving the killing of their intelligence personnel?

In view of the British Government's reaction to these shootings, Collins was more than justified. They accepted after Bloody Sunday that they were dealing with an organized and efficient force and so began their first efforts at negotiation. The British Government overlooked one significant point in their struggle with the Irish Republican Army, and that was the fighting qualities of their opponents. For centuries Irish soldiers had fought courageously and skilfully in the armies of Britain—and against them as well at times—and their virtues in battle had been well acknowledged. British Generals like Wellington, Raglan, Roberts, Haig and even French had all been generous in their praise, but now the Irish—and now fighting for the cause nearest their hearts—were described by the British as faint-hearted, cowardly fellows who shot defenceless police and soldiers from behind walls and hedges. The British forgot that in the struggle for Irish independence in 1798 they had had to use more troops to defeat the Irish than they deployed to defeat Napoleon at Waterloo—of course at Waterloo the Irish were on Wellington's side. It has usually been overlooked by the Anglo-Saxons as well that the same Normans who defeated the English in one battle at Hastings and occupied Britain took 400 years before they could occupy Ireland, and then they had to hold it with armed militia—but that is where we came in!

The Irish started their fight without arms. Never before in the history of wars of independence had the invaded had to depend almost entirely for tools of war on the invaders. An insignificant trickle of rifles and ammunition was smuggled into Ireland for the I R A. The one-shot Howth rifles landed near Dublin before the Dublin rebellion were inefficient and untrustworthy; thousands of rounds of revolver ammunition smuggled from America were too big for the weapons and the I R A's attempts to pare the lead bullets so that they would fit led to accusations that the I R A were using dum-dum bullets. In Cork the I R A had to buy chemicals in twopennyworths from chemists' shops to stuff into the hubs of farm carts to provide dangerous but unpredictable land mines. They had to buy it in small quantities in order to keep within the Act!

The only way the I R A could obtain arms and ammunition in quantity was to capture them from the armed forces they were attacking, and in carrying out these attacks the average amount of rifle ammunition an I R A man carried was five rounds. Home-made hand grenades and ammunition roughly made by amateurs in Dublin cellars and hide-outs in the country districts—much of it unreliable and inaccurate—were used against the products of the best armament factories in the world.

This victory of mind over matter is well illustrated by Jack Aherne's action in a house in Cloyne, Co. Cork. He and a number of other members of I R A were in a derelict house which was surrounded by military. The I R A men kept silent until the two soldiers battered down the door and entered cautiously. The I R A immediately fired at them. The soldiers wisely fled—one of them casting a hand grenade behind him. Aherne accurately calculated the flight of the bomb and as it touched the floor drop-kicked it smartly out through the open door where it exploded. Aherne, delighted with his footwork, subsequently carried on a conversation with a soldier on the other side of the wall of the house. Both Aherne and the British soldier were firing when Aherne called out, "Come and get it, Tommy." "After you, Paddy," replied the soldier politely. Conversation finished when the I R A burst out through another door firing madly, and all of them managed to escape.

The British Government of that day, urged and advised by men whose bigotry engulfed their intelligence, refused to believe that the I R A were anything but scattered gangs of cowardly murderers. They never stopped to think how so much opposition—intelligent and effective opposition—was organized. The Prime Minister, Lloyd George, then the head of a Coalition Government, was also influenced by political motives. To his political ambitions Ireland and the Irish people came a very poor second. He was anticipating the end of the Coalition and the possible position of his own Liberal Party, and he was gambling on, and thinking he was going the right way about, recruiting the support of what was left of the old Irish Nationalist Party. The mind of a professional, power-mad politician is a tortuous, twisted and inhuman machine. Power corrupts and success can breed indifference to the tribulations of lesser mortals. He was both powerful and successful.

No doubt he and his colleagues had read Irish history, which is punctuated by stories of abortive rebellions, but they failed to grasp the difference about this latest one. The Sinn Fein movement differed fundamentally from most of the previous rebellions in that it was a revolution of the ordinary people led by ordinary people, it was a revolution from the bottom not from the top. It was a Catholic revolution in which, for the first time, neither the Protestants nor the Anglo-Irish had an influential part. Previously the revolutionaries were detached from the Irish people by class barriers, the people were pawns.

Sinn Fein, directly descended from the Fenian Movement through the links of the Irish Republican Brotherhood, was the first truly national, truly democratic and truly united movement to challenge British overlordship. That is not to say that it was a purely Catholic movement; many of its most brilliant leaders were not Catholics—Erskine Childers, Robert Barton, Ernest Blythe, to mention a few—and there were many other non-Catholics in the ranks of the I R A throughout the whole of Ireland. It is not necessary to be a Catholic to be a good Irishman—many a Protestant church and family protected members of the I R A and their armaments during the dangerous days and nights of "the terror".

From 1919 until the truce in 1921 Sinn Fein made the British claim, that they were endeavouring to maintain law and order, ridiculous. During that period the British ceased even to try to maintain the normal procedure of civil law and order. The I R A were obliged to set up civil courts because civil offences continued to take place; they were obliged also to set up their own civil police. The utterly fantastic position prevailed of the British police and military acting purely as an occupying terrorist force, while the people they were terrorizing set up their own police force and civil courts.

After Bloody Sunday the war in Ireland increased in intensity. The British became more ferocious—the Irish more calculating. The I R A, now utterly outlawed, expected even less quarter from the British forces than ever before. They became more traditionally guerilla. They roamed the hills in columns, lived in derelict houses in remote places and in dug-outs excavated in fields and mountain sides. They travelled at night to ambush positions and faded away when action finished. The British kept normally to the main roads and avoided the small turnings. Indeed, the British did not know the side roads; the Irish would erect a gate across a side road or hide it with hastily erected stone walls or bushes so that the military and police would pass it by, or think it was a private road leading to a private house.

The I R A intelligence became better as that of the British deteriorated. Eventually British intelligence dried up completely.

The I R A, on the other hand, issued a directive to their provincial leaders that they were to ignore information offered by soldiers or Black and Tans as the need for it had passed. However, if any members of the Crown forces wished to desert they were to be given safe passage out of Ireland.

There are many stories told of the end of the Anglo-Irish war and how it came about. The one that has not been told yet is that it happened through the services of a Nonconformist minister who was not the slightest bit interested in politics.[2] Nonconformists, however, are almost *de facto* rebels, and one of them in Ireland was instructed from a high authority in London to leave out part of his usual Sunday service on a stated Sunday. It was part of the prayers for the King. He did so and after the service was approached by a woman in the congregation whom he did not know, who instructed him to write back to London stating that one of the most important of the Irish leaders (not Michael Collins) would be available for a preliminary discussion in a particular house in Ireland. An important personage duly arrived from London, met this Irish leader and so began the discussions which led to the truce of July 1921.

The truce led to Ireland becoming a Free State but the I R A divided. Some with de Valera, Childers, Cathal Brugha and others refused to accept the British offer; Michael Collins and Arthur Griffith led the Free State side who wished to accept the terms. The Free Staters, with borrowed British artillery, began another fighting war in Ireland—a bitter civil one.

Michael Collins became General Collins of the Free State Army, and one day during an ambush in Co. Cork he was shot dead, some say deliberately, some say accidentally by a random bullet. The greatest of them all was dead and his political enemies as well as his friends mourned him.

Probably the last newspaper reporter to interview Collins before his death was Patrick Murphy, who first met him one dark night in Dublin when Murphy was a young reporter on the *Freeman's Journal*.[3] Murphy, keen and enterprising, had an arrangement with the ambulance drivers who were called to collect bodies found on the streets of Dublin. The ambulance drivers would phone Murphy when they were called, and he would immediately slip into an ambulance attendant's coat and travel with them. He was then in a position to search the body and find out the name and address of the victim. This ruse gave his paper numerous scoops over its rivals and infuriated the British authorities, who were usually responsible for the deaths of civilians, but disliked to see the details appear so quickly in the morning newspaper.

Murphy was returning from such an outing during curfew one night when a lorry load of Auxiliaries drove by. He slipped quickly into a doorway and covered his face with his hat so that the whiteness would not give him away. After the lorry had passed he discovered that another man was standing beside him in the same doorway. "Good evening," said the stranger, "and who would you be?" "Murphy from the *Freeman's Journal*," said Murphy. "I know your people," said the other man, "do you mind if I come in with you?" "Not at all," said Murphy, "come along."

The stranger told him his name was Carrol and he sat down at the desk eyeing a large bottle of Bovril which Murphy had just bought and for which he had a particular taste. They had only been seated a few minutes when Auxiliaries swooped on the building. Murphy ran down the stairs and met three of them coming up with their guns in their hands. The reporter, who had attended school in England, put on his best English accent which he found particularly useful on such occasions and asked them what they wanted. "We want a fellow called Carrol," said the leader. Murphy raised his voice so that the stranger could hear him and replied, "If it's Carrols you want, you have come to the right place. If you want Carrols, we've got them. Come on now and I'll get you plenty of Carrols." When they entered the office Carrol was gone—and so was the bottle of Bovril, Murphy noticed. He led the Auxiliaries down to the basement where there were scores of men working on printing presses and, going to the foreman, he winked and said, "These gentlemen want a man named Carrol—are there any here?" The foreman called out, "All Carrols come forward" —and about fifteen men lined up. The Auxiliaries walked out. When Murphy went back to his office Carrol reappeared and placed an empty Bovril bottle on the desk. "That was lovely," he said, "I was starving." He was then with another member of the staff who knew him and who went to escort him safely off the premises. "That was Mick Collins and he went on the roof during the raid," Murphy was told.

During the Treaty negotiations in London, Murphy, who was then working for the *New York Herald*, met him frequently and—being from the same county as Collins—got on very well with him. When civil war in Ireland became inevitable Collins changed and refused to meet the Press as freely as he used to. Murphy's editor said to him one day, "You know

Collins well. He will not see any Press men—you go and see him and get a story." Murphy went to Collins's hotel in London and as he approached his room saw that he was just saying good-bye to a priest. When Collins saw Murphy he said, "Come in, Paudeen." In the room Murphy noticed a bottle of whisky with a small amount of the liquor missing—he had just given the priest a drink—and an expensive-looking woman's fur coat lying on the bed. Collins would not drink himself but he handed Murphy the bottle and, glancing at the fur coat, said, "I suppose you wonder what that is doing here?" "I was," said Murphy. "It's a breaking-off present for the girl I was going to marry," said Collins, "I must break it off because I don't want her to marry a corpse and I could not think what to give her until your paper sent me a cheque for £500, for a feature they asked me for. I didn't expect it and I've never had so much money before—it came in very handy for the coat."

"What are you talking about—being a corpse?" said Murphy. "They want to get me. And why shouldn't they get me? When I wanted anybody I got them—and I trained the fellows who want me now. They can get me all right," Collins answered.

Patrick Murphy, now a well preserved man who is in charge of one of the most important departments of one of the English daily newspapers, told me how he had overheard Collins say to de Valera in Dublin about that time: "Let us all vote for the Treaty or let us all vote against the Treaty and then go to the Country. I only want to do what the Irish people want and in this way we can find what their wishes are."

Cathal Brugha could have surrendered to the Free State forces and saved his life. He chose to come out of a burning building with a blazing revolver in his hand, ignored orders to surrender, and died through the bullet wounds of his former comrades. Erskine Childers was executed by the Free State forces in November 1922. Six armed soldiers had rushed into his room to capture him. Childers drew his revolver to resist but a woman ran in front of him shouting, "You are not to shoot, Mr Childers." He would not fire in case she was shot so he dropped his gun. An hour before he died he wrote, "It all seems perfectly simple and inevitable, like lying down after a long day's work."

The dreadful story of the Irish Civil War has yet to be told in detail. We are concerned only with the fight for independence—the fight that finished in July 1921. As far as Britain is concerned it was the first of many successful rebellions against their rule. The fight by the Irish taught many other peoples how to prosecute a successful guerilla war against British forces. It became a "copy book" war for countries like Israel and Cyprus who learned from it how to use inferior forces in order to make rule impossible by much superior forces. The British—*mirabile dictu*—learned nothing from their defeat in Ireland. The reports from Israel and Cyprus in later years read very similarly to those which appeared in the newspapers between 1919 and 1921 concerning Ireland, and inevitably, after reactions by the forces of the Crown very similar to their reactions in Ireland, the British left. Maybe you cannot teach an old dog new tricks or perhaps the leopard does not change its spots! How can such a pleasant people as the British earn, and deservedly earn, such a disreputable reputation in the treatment of people of smaller nations who seek independence for themselves? Nobody can blame the British for wanting to maintain their interests in Ireland—it is a pleasant country and the fishing and shooting are excellent— but it is difficult to understand the mentality of certain classes of the British who condemned the "damn' rebel Irish" for wishing to run and rule their own country.

Bloody Sunday is long past. It was one of the most dreadful days in the long painful history of Britain's armed occupation of its sister isle and of Britain's mail-fisted efforts to create a subject race. It is important because the morning was marked by an operation essential to the aims of the Irish Republican Army and the afternoon tarnished by an operation symbolic of the whole sad story of British occupation.

In July 1922, British forces left.

SOURCES

1 *The Easter Lily*, by Sean O'Callaghan.
2 *Constabulary Gazette*, June 1920.
3 *The Easter Lily*, by Sean O'Callaghan.
4 The late Tom Hancock.
5 The account of the fighting about the Law Courts was given by Jack Shouldice and confirmed by a subsequent document prepared by the Battalion Officers giving the personal stories of the survivors.
6 James Kenny's personal account.

CHAPTER 3

1 Jack Shouldice's report and a private source.

CHAPTER 4

1 *The life of Sean Tracey*, by D. Ryan.
2 *Constabulary Gazette*, May 1920.
3 *Constabulary Gazette*, April 1920.
4 *Constabulary Gazette*, February 1921.
5 *Constabulary Gazette*, February 1920.
6 *Ireland for Ever*, by Brigadier General Crozier.
7 *Daily Mirror*, 15 November, 1921.
8 Private source.
9 *The Easter Lily*, by Sean O'Callaghan.

CHAPTER 6

1 Tom Barry's own account in *Rebel Cork's Fighting Story*, published by *The Kerryman*.
2 *Constabulary Gazette*, September 1920.
3 *Four Glorious Years*, by David Hogan.
4 Account by Florence O'Donoghue in *Rebel Cork's Fighting Story*, published by *The Kerryman*.
5 James O'Beirne's own account.
6 George Gormby's own account.
7 *Ireland for Ever*, by Brigadier General Crozier.
8 The account of the sacking of Cork City is from newspaper accounts of the time and a description of that night by Florence O'Donoghue in *Rebel Cork's Fighting Story*.
9 *Daily News*, 1 November, 1920.
10 *Daily News*, 27 July, 1920.

CHAPTER 7

1 Private source.
2 *Winter's Tale*, by Sir Ormonde Winter.
3 Sir Ormonde tells this story in *Winter's Tale* and Ernie O'Malley in *On Another Man's Wound* mentioned a "broken spirited" fellow prisoner he met in Kilmainham gaol who, he was told, jumped from a soldier's lorry, handcuffed, whilst being driven from the gaol to Dublin Castle. This was the same man.
4 *Four Glorious Years*, by David Hogan.
5 Sir Ormonde Winter tells his side of the story in *Winter's Tale* and David Hogan corrects him in *Four Glorious Years*.
6 *Sean Tracey*, by D. Ryan.
7 *Daily News*, 18 October, 1920.
8 *Irish Bulletin* and *Four Glorious Years*.
9 Ernie O'Malley's own story in *On Another Man's Wound*.
10 Piaras Beaslai.
11 *Ourselves Alone*, by Padraic Colum.
12 *The Times*, 19 November, 1920.
13 *The Times*, 27 November, 1920.
14 *Daily News*, 13 October, 1920.
15 *Daily News*, 20 October, 1920.
16 and 17 *Daily News*, 28 October, 1920.
18 Richard Bennett's account in the *New Statesman*, 24 March, 1961.
19 Private source.
20 *Irish Independent*, 16 November, 1920.
21 *Four Glorious Years*, by David Hogan.
22 *With the Dublin Brigade*, by Charles Dalton.

CHAPTER 8

1 Events described in this chapter are taken in the first place from the reports which appeared in the morning and evening papers in London and Dublin on Monday, 22 November, 1920. The stories differed only in the very slightest details from paper to paper. These reports have been confirmed and extended through the personal accounts of the men involved in the incidents.
2 Private source.
3 *Ireland for Ever*, by Brigadier General Crozier.
4 James Kenny's own account.
5 Eileen's own account.

CHAPTER 9

1 Jack Shouldice's own account.
2 *The Big Sycamore*, by Joseph Brady.
3 Private source.
4 *The Times*, 22 November, 1920.
5 Private source.

CHAPTER 10

1 Ernie O'Malley's description in *Dublin's Fighting Story*, published by *The Kerryman*.
2 This communiqué appeared in the newspapers of 23 November, 1920.

CHAPTER 11

1 *Morning Post*, 22 November, 1920.
2 Private source.
3 *Daily News*, 22 November, 1920.
4 *The Times*, 22 November, 1920.
5 *The Times*, 24 November, 1920.
6 *Daily News*, 23 November, 1920.
7 *Manchester Guardian*, 22 November, 1920.
8 *Morning Post*, 22 November, 1920.
9 *The Times*, 23 November, 1920.
10 *Daily Mirror*, 23 November, 1920.

CHAPTER 12

1 *Daily Telegraph*, 26 November, 1920.
2 *Daily Express*, 26 November, 1920.
3 *Irish Independent*, 26 November, 1920.
4 *Evening News*, 26 November, 1920.
5 *Spectator*, 26 November, 1920.
6 *Spectator*, 26 November, 1920.
7 *Spectator*, 2 December, 1920.
8 *Spectator*, 17 December, 1920.
9 *Spectator*, 23 December, 1920.
10 *Michael Collins*, by Rex Taylor.
11 Ernie O'Malley in *On Another Man's Wound* and the personal account of Simon Donnelly.
12 *Daily News*, 22 November, 1920.
13 *Westminster Gazette*, 18 February, 1921.
14 *The Times*, 29 January, 1921.

CHAPTER 13

1 *The Irish at the Front*, by Michael MacDonagh.
2 Private source.
3 Pat Murphy's own account.